A Story of Jesus' Life

Based on the Apocryphal Gospels

Antonio Piñero
Thomas W. Hudgins

Energion Publications
Cantonment, FL
2024

Cover Design: Henry Neufeld

ISBN: 978-1-63199-881-2
eISBN: 978-1-63199-882-9
Library of Congress Control Number: 2024931755

Energion Publications
1241 Conference Rd
Cantonment, FL 32533

pubs@energion.com
energion.com

TABLE OF CONTENTS

Abbreviations

Old Testament Pseudepigrapha

1 En.	*1 Enoch*
Cav. Tr.	*Cave of Treasures*
L.A.E.	*Life of Adam and Eve*
Sib. Or.	*Sibylline Oracles*
T. Ab.	*Testament of Abraham*
T. Benj.	*Testament of Benjamin*
T. Levi	*Testament of Levi*
T. 12. Patr.	*Testaments of the Twelve Patriarchs*

Apocrypha and Septuagint

Bel	*Bel and the Dragon*

New Testament Apocrypha and Pseudepigrapha

Acts Andr. Matt.	*Acts of Andrew and Matthias*
Acts John	*Acts of John*
Acts Pet.	*Acts of Peter*
Acts Pil.	*Acts of Pilate*
(Arab.) Gos. Inf.	*Arabic Gospel of the Infancy*
(Arm.) Gos. Inf.	*Armenian Gospel of the Infancy*
Ascen. Isa.	*Ascension of Isaiah*
Acts Pet.	*Acts of Peter*
Acts Pet. Paul	*Acts of Peter and Paul (Acta Petri et Pauli)*
Acts Thom.	*Acts of Thomas*
Act. Verc.	*Actus Vercellenses*
Anaph. Pil.	*Anaphora of Pilate*
B. Inf. Sav.	*Book of the Infancy of the Savior (Liber de infantia salvatoris)*
(Cop.) Gos. Heb.	*Coptic Gospel of the Hebrews*
Desc. Chr. ad. Inf.	*Descent of Christ to Hell (Descensus Christi ad Inferos)*

v

Desc. Mary	*Descent of Mary (Genna Marias)*
Ep. Apost.	*Epistula Apostolorum*
(Eth.) B. Rest	*Ethiopian Book of Rest*
Gos. Bart.	*Gospel of Bartholomew*
Gos. Bir. Mary	*Gospel of the Birth of Mary*
	(De nativitate Mariae)
Gos. Eb.	*Gospel of the Ebionites*
Gos. Eg.	*Gospel of the Egyptians*
Gos. Eve	*Gospel of Eve*
Gos. Jud.	*Gospel of Judas*
Gos. Marcion	*Gospel of Marcion*
Gos. Mary	*Gospel of Mary*
Gos. Naz.	*Gospel of the Nazarenes*
Gos. Nic.	*Gospel of Nicodemus*
	(Descent of Christ into Hell)
Gos. Pet.	*Gospel of Peter*
Gos. Phil.	*Gospel of Philip*
Gos. Thom.	*Gospel of Thomas*
Hist. Jos. Carp.	*History of Joseph the Carpenter*
	(Historia Josephi Fabri Lignari)
Jos. of Arim.	*Narrative of Joseph of Arimathea*
Mem. Apost.	*Memoria Apostolorum*
Prot. James	*Protoevangelium of James*
Ps.-Mt.	*Gospel of Pseudo-Matthew*
Ps.-Thom.	*Gospel of Pseudo-Thomas*
Sec. Gos. Mk.	*Secret Gospel of Mark*
Soph. Jes. Chr.	*Sophia of Jesus Christ*
	(Sophia Jesu Christi)
(Syr.) Did. Apost.	*Didascalia Apostolorum*
	(Syriac)

Dead Sea Scrolls

1QH	*Hodayot or Thanksgiving Hymns*
1QTem	*Temple Scroll*

Introduction

The earliest communities of Jesus followers were focused on studying a very narrow record of Jesus' life. The earliest Gospels focused more than a third of their content on the last week of Jesus' life. Of these accounts recognized as "authoritative" and accurately documenting or faithfully representing the life and works of Jesus, the last one written spent about the same amount of space covering the 24-hour period surrounding the crucifixion— Jesus' final afternoon and evening with his closest disciples, his arrest and trial, and his crucifixion and death on the cross. The events surrounding Jesus' life were important, but in the eyes of these communities and the authors of their earliest texts, the single most important event in Jesus' life was his death on the cross and his resurrection two mornings later. Everything else in Matthew, Mark, Luke, and John is designed to reinforce the significance of Jesus' death.

The details surrounding Jesus' lineage, birth, and infancy are few in comparison to the amount concerning his final three years. They are necessary—Jesus is presented as human in each, and human characters have family trees, birth stories, and childhoods. Jesus is no exception. Little was written about his comings and goings, but not because little was known. Mary would have been able to supply all the details curious minds wanted to know about Jesus' early years. So, why was so little written in the earliest Gospels? —Because Jesus' life was quite normal prior to his baptism in the Jordan River by his cousin John. Luke, for example, recounted a story of Jesus' parents departing Jerusalem after observing the Passover but unaware that Jesus had not accompanied them (Luke 2:41–44). When they returned to Jerusalem, they found Jesus "in the temple, sitting in the midst of the teachers, both listening to them and asking questions" (Luke 2:46). And this nicely parallels what Luke says just a little earlier: "The child continued to grow and become strong, being filled with wisdom; and the grace of God was upon him" (Luke 2:40). Naturally, how does someone learn? – They ask questions. They observe. They think critically. Jesus, Paul would later tell the Philippians, willfully chose to not exercise his divine attributes during his incarnation (Phil. 2:6–7). He needed the grace of God over his life as much as any other child growing up in the first century. He needed to ask questions as much as any other child. He needed to listen as much as any other child. He needed to grow mentally, physically, and emotionally.

Something changed with Jesus' baptism. No miracles took place prior to that event. And it is the reason that Luke refers to the beginning of Jesus' ministry immediately after this event (Luke 3:23). At Jesus' baptism, the Holy Spirit descends from heaven like a dove and comes upon Jesus, language reminiscent of the presence of the Holy Spirit in the lives of the prophets (Luke 3:22). And this is why Jesus would later tell people that he was willing and able to forgive any sin except "blasphemy against the Spirit" (Matt. 12:31). And while there have been many interpretations about what Jesus meant by that expression, the context is rather clear. The religious leaders attributed his healings and miracles to the power of Satan when, in fact, as Jesus knew, they were done by the power of the one who descended upon him at his baptism. And Jesus, who has the authority to forgive sins or not, decided to not forgive a group of people for ascribing miracles performed by the power of the Holy Spirit falsely and incorrectly to the power of Satan. That whole account is another indication that these earliest Gospels had very little to write about concerning the infancy, youth, and young adulthood of Jesus. Were they unique? Sure, as much as the story of anyone's childhood is unique compared to someone else's. But they were for the most part uneventful compared to all that transpired in the last few years of Jesus' life from the Jordan River to Golgotha.

And in very short time the accounts of Matthew, Mark, Luke, and John were not enough. Curiosities began to form about what Jesus' childhood was like. We could even call it a "quest" to fill in the gaps. Doctrinal issues arose about Jesus' divine attributes, and communities were wrestling with what that must have looked like in Jesus' infancy and childhood. And there were questions about what Mary's life must have been like—Was she always a virgin? Did she ever sin? Was her only role in God's salvific plan bearing Jesus in her womb or did/does she have a mediatory role between the world and Jesus? Sometimes these questions and curiosities were addressed via treatises or councils, but other times we find them addressed in art and literature. In many cases these apocryphal texts are evidence of what Christians or sects believed and worshipped.

The texts used to construct this story of Jesus' life were not admitted into the New Testament canon. They come from many different places in the Mediterranean and were not written at the exact same time. They range from the mid-second century AD—although the Gospel of Peter might have been written earlier (c. AD 130)—and the mid-eighth century AD (e.g., some of the texts that tell the story of Mary's assumption into heaven). With that said, those given a later date might have been preserved or developed from stories and traditions that date much earlier, perhaps the third or fourth centuries.

Nevertheless, these works are all far removed in time from the events they narrate. As a result, their authors are continuously carried off by fantasy and imagination. The apocryphal Gospels offer many details of the life of Jesus that do not appear in the earliest Gospels. By putting them together and synthesizing them, we can draw a picture of his life that is full and rich in detail. But it is quite another thing to accept them as historical. It is important to remember that these texts were never harmonized in the same way that the canonical texts were harmonized, beginning with Tatian's *Diatessaron* in the second century AD. This book, so far as we know, is the first and only attempt to harmonize the apocryphal accounts, the primary goal being to give readers a user-friendly introduction to their contents. For those who have no idea what the Jesus of the apocryphal texts was like (and probably more correct to say the Jesuses [plural]), they can read this one story. Many times, these sources contain information that is just impossible to harmonize; they are simply contradictory. In such cases, when the details are muddled, we have chosen to go with the general storyline, or the one the evidence tends to suggest. Footnotes are provided so that the reader can trace statements and narrative accounts back their apocryphal source of origin.

The focus of the book is to present how Jesus is portrayed in apocryphal texts. The goal is not to reproduce the apocryphal texts themselves. For that, readers should consult in English: Bart D. Ehrman and Zlatko Pleše's *The Apocryphal Gospels: Texts and Translations* (Oxford: Oxford University Press, 2011) and J. K. Elliott's *The Apocryphal New Testament: A Collection of Apocryphal Christian Literature in an English Translation* (Oxford: Clarendon, 2005). Hopefully, this introduction will spark in the readers more and more interest. These texts might have been hidden for centuries, but they are readily accessible to anyone today. And while they do not point exactly to the Jesus of history, they offer much to consider regarding the worship of Jesus through history into the present day.

Thomas W. Hudgins

A Story of Jesus' Life
Based on the Apocryphal Gospels

Mary the Chosen

According to the old records of the twelve tribes of Israel, there lived in Jerusalem a very wealthy young man whose name was Joachim; he feared God, and his godliness was unsurpassed in those days. His offerings in the temple were always twice that of everyone else[1] and of his property usually thrice; despite having very much, he lived with very little, distributing the rest among widows, orphans, the poor, and the priests that served in the temple. God rewarded him by doubling his property, so much that he came to own large flocks. When he was twenty years old, he married Anna, the daughter of Issachar, who belonged to the same tribe: they were both descendants of David. After twenty years of marriage though, they still had no children.[2]

The great day of the Feast of the Harvest came to pass in autumn. During that time, the Law of God was read to the people and tabernacles of straw and branches were constructed, like the ones usually found in gardens. This resembled the period in Israel's history when they were in the desert, and they celebrated this way in order to remember their covenant with God and that they were but sojourners in a land graciously given to them by God. Joachim went up to the temple one day during the feast to offer his gifts.[3] Then Issachar the priest, once he noticed that Joachim mingled with men who had children, rebuked him: "It is not lawful for

---

1   *Prot. James* 1:1.

2   *Ps.-Mt.* 1.

3   *Prot. James* 1:2.

you to offer your offerings first, because you have not produced a child. God probably thinks you are unworthy of having a child. If you search the Scriptures well, you will see that God declares people like you accursed in Israel."[4]

Needless to say, Joachim was embarrassed and perplexed by the insult hurled at him by Issachar in the presence of so many people. In fact, there was no passage in the Law that justified such an outburst, and it simply could not be defended. Joachim withdrew, nearly dead from shame and completely without words. He went and consulted some records and realized that the great characters of Israel's history had not been condemned to infertility. All of them had children, one way or another. Faced with this news, he did not even dare to appear before his wife. Instead, afflicted, weary, and sad, he withdrew to a desert-like region where the flocks were grazing. He pitched his tent there, next to those of his laborers, and he fasted for forty days and forty nights. He told himself: "I will not eat until God visits me. My prayers will be my food and drink."[5] Five months passed, and his wife Anna had not seen him. She was like a widow during that period.

The good woman lived between sobs. She raised her voice to heaven and complained to God with these words: "Why after refusing to give me any children, would you also take away my husband? Five months have passed, and I have not seen him. I do not even know if he is dead. If I did, I could at least bury him." In despair, she entered the court of their home, and she saw some sparrows sitting in their nest in a laurel tree. The sight of those little creatures made her burst into bitter lamentation: "Almighty God! You—who have given offspring to every creature, to the birds, the beasts of the earth, the fish in the water—will I be the only one from whom you withhold your kindness? You know the vow I made when I married. If you had given me a son or a daughter, I would have offered them in your holy temple."[6]

---

4   *Gos. Bir. Mary* 2:2.

5   *Prot. James* 1:4.

6   *Ps.-Mt.* 2:2.

Her maiden, Judith, with whom she had the most confidence and who knew perfectly well of her shame, tried to comfort her. She tried to cheer her up and said: "As you know, we have a big party planned. How long will you be humiliated in your soul? Change your clothes. Touch your head with this handkerchief that the owner of a loom gave me—which I cannot bear, for I am not free—and rejoice."

But Anna initially refused. She was soon persuaded, though, and changed her clothes in mourning, went down from her chambers to the garden, and began to walk to relieve her pain.[7] Then, an angel of God suddenly appeared before her. He said: "Do not be afraid, Anna, nor think this is a ghost in your sight. I am the angel who presented your prayers to God. The Almighty has determined that you will bear a child, who will be the object of admiration forever until the end of the ages."[8]

The angel also promised that her offspring would be devoted to the service of the Lord in the temple of the holy city, at the time and place of God's choosing. But Anna just could not believe it, and she was scared and trembling at having seen what she saw. She lay on her bed and stayed there all day and all night, praying and crying even more,[9] wondering if she had really heard and saw all that had transpired.

About the same time there appeared a certain young man wandering in the mountains where Joachim had put his flocks to graze. He approached and said to him: "Why do you not return to your wife?"

Though he did not know the young man, Joachim felt like he could trust him he explained his reasons for not returning, insisting that it was the reproach of infertility. The young man replied: "Do not worry. I am an angel of God. I have even visited your wife today. The Lord has heard your prayer. Your wife shall conceive and bear a blessed child. No one will be able to liken it

---

7   *Prot. James* 2:3.

8   *Gos. Bir. Mary* 3:1–2.

9   *Ps.-Mt.* 2:4.

to anything. Even in the future, they will find nothing to compare it to, I can promise you that. Go down from these mountains and run to your wife's side."

Joachim stood there stunned for a moment, but then reacted quickly. He believed what the angel had said and invited the angel to stay with him a little longer, to eat at his table. The angel refused, arguing that the food of angels was very different. But because he felt generous, he could offer to God as a sacrifice whatever he would spend at the banquet. Joachim did just that, and he ordered that ten lambs and twelve calves be brought to him. Having offered the sacrifice, together with the fragrance and smoke the angel rose up to heaven.[10] Joachim promptly undid his tent and set off for home.

Shortly after these things happened, two messengers arrived with a message for Anna: "Make haste, and hurry to the Golden Gate, for Joachim, your husband, is back with his flocks. An angel of the Lord has visited him and promised him that you will conceive a child in your womb."

Anna was waiting at the door as Joachim arrived with his entourage of shepherds and flocks. When she saw her husband in the dust, she ran and leaped to his neck, excited and trembling. She said: "Now I see that God has blessed me abundantly, because I will cease being a widow and I will conceive in my womb."[11]

Her husband also embraced her tenderly and went with her. And Joachim rested that night with his wife at home.

Anna soon noticed the natural signs of pregnancy. Joachim, full of joy, called one of his shepherds and ordered him: "Bring me ten unblemished lambs, for the temple of the Lord, and twelve milk cows, for the priests and the Sanhedrin. To the people I will make a gift of a hundred goatlings."

The next day his servants hauled these gifts to the temple. The people who were assembled there felt admiration and they blessed Joachim: "Praise be to the God of Israel who has fulfilled

10   *Ps.-Mt.* 3:2–4.

11   *Prot. James* 4:4.

your wishes." The good man, now before the priest as his offerings were sacrificed, vowed that his child would be consecrated to God. "Lord of Israel," he said in his heart, "since you have heard your servant, I will give back to you whatever you grant me, whether a boy or a girl. He or she will stay in your temple, serving you, for his or her whole life." When the priest was about to slay the last lamb on the altar, a huge miracle happened: The knife penetrated deep into the soft neck of the animal, but it did not shed blood, but white milk instead. The priest, inspired by the Spirit, made the following prophecy to Joachim: "This milk that flows from the artery is a sign that your offspring will be a girl, a spotless and holy virgin who will be the mother of the king of Israel."

The sacrifice concluded and Joachim went home. The days passed peacefully, and the time came for Anna to give birth; without pain or contraction she gave birth in the quietest room of the house. She asked the midwife: "What I have brought into the world?" She replied: "You have given birth to a beautiful, radiant, and splendid daughter, without any blemish." Anna felt an immense joy, like a fire burning inside her. And then she raised her voice and said: "Blessed be the God of Israel who has heard the pleas of his servants."

Anna started to breastfeed, and the baby grew day by day. It was necessary to give the girl a name, but they found none that suited them. One day an angel visited Joachim and Anna and told them that the divinely appointed name for the girl was Mary, which means "exalted by God"[12] in Hebrew, the language of creation.[13] Joachim did so with joy and gave his daughter the name Mary. After forty days, Anna performed the necessary purification, according to the customary laws. Then she and her husband came to the temple and presented the child before God.[14]

As time progressed, Mary got stronger. When she was six months old, her mother put her down on the ground. The girl

---

12   *1 En.* 60.
13   *B. Inf. Sav.* 16.
14   *(Arm.) Gos. Inf.* 2:2–7.

already knew how to walk perfectly; she took a few small steps and returned to her mother's lap. And she said: "You are extraordinary. As sure as God lives, you will not take another step on ordinary floor before you are taken to the temple, whose floor is holy." Anna then ordered that a chapel be built in her room, which was very spacious, so that the child could play, but also pass the time in a godly way, not allowing unclean things to pass through her hands. She called several Hebrew maidens, and they were hired with an impressive salary to care for and entertain Mary. In order to mark this first year, Joachim decided to celebrate the anniversary with a beautiful feast, to which he invited the priests, scribes, the whole Sanhedrin, and the more prominent people of the village. One could say that all Jerusalem had gathered at her house. The girl was brought in so that everyone could lay their eyes on her. And the priests heaped blessing upon blessing upon her. One of them said aloud: "O God Almighty! Set your eyes on this girl and grant a special blessing, one so great there would be no need for any blessings in the future." Anna, on the way to breastfeed her daughter, was overjoyed and exclaimed to herself: "Who is going to say to the children of Reuben that Anna, the barren one, is breastfeeding? Hear, hear all the tribes of Israel— Anna is breastfeeding!" After laying the girl down to rest, she returned to be with the dinner guests. The banquet ended and all were rejoicing and praising the God of Israel.[15]

To mark Mary's second year, Joachim wanted to fulfill his promise and he proposed to his wife that they take the child to the temple. Anna, however, did not agree, thinking that Mary was too young and might miss her home and parents. Joachim respected her decision, so they waited another year. After that, when Mary had just turned three, she was taken to the temple. Since her father was an important figure, several Hebrew girls accompanied the girl on her way to the temple, carrying candles in their hands. It was not something people saw everyday, so the people of Jerusalem flooded the streets to watch the procession. Once they

15   *Prot. James* 6:1–3.

arrived at the temple, Joachim and Anna offered sacrifices and entrusted Mary to the high priest, so she could dwell among a group of virgins from wealthy families—especially those from the tribe of Judah and the line of David.[16] These virgins spent their lives praising and serving God until the time came for them to assume another role. Mary was taken to the front of the temple, and she climbed the fifteen steps so quickly that she had no time to look back and say goodbye to her parents. All were amazed, even the priests themselves: so small, so determined, so devoted to the Lord.

God rewarded the generosity of Joachim and Anna. Not long after, Anna became pregnant again and gave birth to another beautiful girl. They named her Mary as well. This Mary would later become the wife of Cleopas.[17]

Some time passed, and near the end of the girl's fifth year of life, Joachim and Anna died. Their relatives handled the burial and organized a large procession to commemorate their lives. They also cared for the second Mary, who was orphaned at such a young age. The first Mary, the mother of Jesus, was deeply saddened at the loss of her parents and mourned their deaths for thirty days.[18]

She was the admiration of the people. God granted her grace and wisdom. In fact, an angel from heaven cared for her and served her continuously, protecting her from any harm. Despite her young age, she walked with a firm step and participated fervently in the divine praises, prayers, and pleas for Israel. Everyone considered them exemplary. Her face shone like snow caressed by the sun, while it was difficult to fix one's gaze upon her. She was also good with her hands, and she produced wool and silk better than many women. She slept only a few hours and spent most of the night in diligent vigils. In the mornings, she used to divvy up her time between manual labor and prayer. It seemed as if Mary's life would later be used as a model for Christian hermits

---

16   (Arm.) Gos. Inf. 4:3.
17   John 19:25.
18   (Arm.) Gos. Inf. 3:2.

and monks. Among the virgins of the temple, Mary stood out in her readiness to follow the instructions of the priests, to recite the psalms with eloquence, to be perfect in virtue. It is said that she was resolved and unchangeable in purpose, and she showed her spirit always the same. No one ever heard a word out of tune or a sentence of gossip or contempt uttered from her lips. Although her peers did not know for sure, they suspected that Mary was fed sustenance brought to her by angels.[19] And to the poor, who frequently gathered at the door of the sanctuary, she handed out the food that was dedicated to the priests. There are also stories that if anyone was sick and touched just the hem of her dress, they were healed.[20] So, Mary approached twelve years of age, and the ungodly could not imagine anything reprehensible in her and considered her behavior worthy of admiration.

Just before she turned twelve, Mary received a visit from a special angel. There was an earthquake on the temple mount, one so strong it nearly tore the veil that separated the Holy of Holies from the rest of the temple. Mary fell to the ground, but the angel held out his hand, raised her up, and said to her: "Hail, chosen vessel."

Then he banged his right hand and there appeared a very large pan, which he placed on the altar of the temple. The angel ate first, and then he gave some food to Mary. He hit the left border of his robe to reveal a chalice filled with wine. He drank first, and then he gave wine to Mary. The angel spoke: "In a few years I will visit you again, and great wonders will be accomplished in you, because you are a chosen vessel for the world." And with these words the angel disappeared.

When the virgins in the temple turned twelve, they were considered old enough to be married. They were to return to their homes and be given in marriage according to the customs of the nation. All the maidens humbly submitted to this requirement, but Mary flat out refused. She told the high priest that she was

19   *Gos. Bart.* 2:15.
20   *Ps.-Mt.* 6:3.

consecrated by the will of her parents (and her own) to the absolute service of God, and she wanted to complete this provision by a vow of perpetual virginity. Neither human force nor the appeal of a man could cause her to break this vow and submit to the yoke of marriage. When the priest heard all of this, it did not sit well with him. On the one hand, such a vow was permitted in Scripture,[21] but on the other hand, he did not want to introduce a new practice in the village. Not only that, but, according to the whole Israelite tradition, marrying and having children was an obligation to the God of their ancestors; in this way new children of the covenant were generated, and the people of Israel became great, increasing their strength among the Gentiles. To not marry and bear children, even though the alternative was wholehearted devotion to the Almighty, was considered an intolerable deviation from what was expected.[22]

In fact, the high priest, whose name was Abiathar, had seen Mary and was intent on giving her in marriage to his son. To make it happen he had distributed substantial gifts between his colleagues, so that they would consent to his wishes. But Mary directly opposed. On one occasion she specifically said: "I will not know a man, nor will any know me, according to my vow."

The priest tried to persuade her, saying: "God is honored by children; the posterity of men is the glory of God, just like it has always been observed in Israel." Mary replied: "In Scripture there are also cases of fair virgins. Abel, for example, pleased God with his offerings and was murdered by his brother before producing any offspring. He knew no woman. Elijah was taken to heaven in his chariot by the Spirit, and yet on earth he did not leave any posterity. A virgin can also be pleasing to the eyes of God. I have resolved in my heart to not know any man."[23]

Mary continued her life in the temple, devoting even more time to the study of the Law, which was unusual in Israel. She

---

21   Ps 75:12.

22   *Gos. Bir. Mary* 7:2.

23   *Ps.-Mt.* 7.

was meditating daily on the texts of the prophets and becoming better known for her daily prayer and reflection on the secrets of the Torah.[24] That approach was unknown in Israel, where women were not considered worthy, due to their lower nature, to devote themselves to the study of the Law. Only men were given to such studies.

After two years, this situation became untenable. The priests asked each other: "What shall we do with Mary? We are fearful at what will happen when the fullness of her womanhood comes, the time of her purification, that it will render the temple unclean without us even noticing." Mary was still virgin and had not started menstruating. It was a very old custom, according to the Law, that prohibited a woman from dwelling in the temple, since her blood would make the place impure. The priests, both Sadducees and Pharisees, were pushing for a decision to be made. Some of them raised their questions to God hoping that he would offer her a solution to this problem. But God remained silent for the moment.

A few days passed and the high priest came again to pray and seek God. God finally agreed to give an answer to the many prayers. A deep and powerful voice from heaven said: "The prophecy foretold by the mouth of my servant Isaiah shall be fulfilled: 'There shall come forth a shoot from the stump of Jesse, and a branch from his roots shall bear fruit. On him will rest the Spirit of the Lord.'"[25] But they did not fully understand what this all meant. So, Abiathar the high priest (others say it was not Abiathar, but Zacharias, the father of John the Baptist, the one that would be the forerunner of the Messiah)[26] entered the Holy of Holies and again asked God for a more accurate indication as how to how they should act in this matter. An angel of the Lord appeared to him and said these words: "Abiathar, depart from her and gather together with all the widowers from the tribe of Judah.

24   Cf. Origen, *Homily VI to Luke*.
25   Isa 11:1.
26   *Prot. James* 8:3.

Let each man come with a staff, and I will indicate with a sign the one to whom I have decided to give this virgin."

The high priest did as God commanded, and heralds went through all the land of Judea sounding trumpets to summon all the widowers in the region. In obedience, they gathered the second day on the temple mount, each man with his staff.

There stood one, confused among the large number of widowers. His name was Joseph. He was advanced in years, a man from the house and family of David. He had six children, four boys and two girls, from a previous marriage.[27]

Saddened by the untimely death of his wife, whom he deeply loved, he had not wanted to remarry. During that time, he lived near the capital, in Bethlehem, a nice little town in the Judean desert. He was fully devoted to his children and his work. He had a workshop where he did everything that was necessary for the construction of houses: from furniture and beds, tools for working in the field, yokes and plows,[28] all the way to the adobe bricks that were used for walls. Business was good; he could not complain because his family was taken care of. He often had to leave Bethlehem for a few days, sometimes even weeks, to personally supervise projects for out-of-towners that flocked to his workshop. Joseph also had an orchard and a vineyard that produced lots of fruit. From time to time he was busy caring for the trees and their fruit (for his own consumption, not trading).[29] Obedient to the call of the priest, the old man went to the temple but with serious reservation, not wanting to further complicate his life.

The priest asked each man for his staff, and they went inside the temple. It was near the end of the day. The afternoon had already passed, and all the hustle and bustle at the temple had dissipated as well. The priests remained in the temple praying all night, and the widowers were outside, some dozing off and others praying. On the following morning, having completed the pledge,

---

27   *Hist. Jos. Carp.* 2:1.

28   Justin, *Dialogue with Trypho* 88.

29   *Pistis Sophia* 61.

Abiathar collected the staffs and asked each man for his name. After marking each staff with a mark, he returned them to their respective owners. Nothing happened. Everyone had been waiting for a sign from above. Right when Joseph took the last staff, behold, out of it came of a beautiful flower, the smell from which, even though they were outside, flooded the atmosphere around it.[30] Right then, the most beautiful dove, whiter than snow, came out of it. After hovering just above the temple, it began to flap its wings over Joseph's head. The priest exclaimed with joy: "To you has fallen the good fortune to receive the virgin of the Lord."

But Joseph was not at all happy with the news, which sounded to him like something that might seriously complicate his life. He answered the priest: "I charge all of the priests and people. Do not force me to do this. How can I oppose something you tell me to do? But I have a large family, children of my own, and I will be ashamed in their presence if I welcome this maiden into my home." They replied: "Fulfill what appears to be the will of God." But Joseph added: "I am old. I could very well die soon. Moreover, what has fallen to me is but a girl, not a woman; everyone would laugh at me."

The high priest appealed to Joseph: "We all know you are a righteous man and have righteous intentions. You know this virgin is an orphan and cannot stay any longer in the temple. Accept the lot that has fallen to you. Take her from us and go with our blessing. Care for her in holiness and honor in accordance with the Law and our traditions, until it comes time to receive the blessed crown that is reserved for you."

But Joseph continued grumbling and offering new arguments before the people and the high priest. He countered that he had come and assembled, but that he had no idea what it was all about. Joseph defended himself: "I did not really know what was going on here. I got lost in my own thoughts and I did not even figure out what was happening."

---

30 *Gos. Bir. Mary* 7:4.

Tired of so much opposition, the priest spoke up in a serious tone: "Fear the Lord and do not resist his provisions. Remember how God behaved with Korah, Dathan, and Abiram, how they were swallowed up by the earth and perished.[31] Be careful that the same does not happen to you as well for opposing his plan."[32]

When Joseph heard this threat, he bowed, took Mary, and he went home. As was the Jewish custom, the preparations for their betrothal began, although no particular feast was celebrated due to the abnormal way they came to be betrothed. In fact, she had only been placed in his care. It was under this condition that he brought Mary to his home for them to live under one roof.

A few days after these events happened, the priests in Jerusalem decided they needed to weave a new veil for the temple. It was a beautiful curtain that separated the Holy of Holies, the most intimate and lovely area of the sanctuary, from the surrounding area, called "holy." The daughters of the house of Judah were assembled and lots were cast among to see who would weave the different portions of the veil: hyacinth, flax, or scarlet. It was an honor to participate in the preparation of such an adornment of the sanctuary. To Mary fell the latter, the scarlet, which was what every girl wanted. The virgins murmured and made jokes about Mary's unending luck. She silently took her work and went home to weave her part.[33] Some time passed, and Joseph sold his home in Bethlehem and moved to Nazareth in Galilee for work, taking Mary with him. The city, though small, was near the Decapolis, populated by many nationalities, and the prospects for his business seemed better there. Joseph's youngest children, James and Simeon—the only ones who still lived with him—moved with him and Mary as well.[34] Mary looked after them like a mother, because they were still very young. This is the reason

---

31   Num 16:1ff.

32   (Arm.) Gos. Inf. 4:3.

33   (Arm.) Gos. Inf. 4:7.

34   As far as who accompanied Joseph, the sources sometimes point to James and other times to Simeon.

why she was called the "mother of James" (and his other brothers), although she was not actually their mother,[35] nor the mother of the other brothers of Jesus.[36]

---

35   *Hist. Jos. Carp.* 4:4.
36   *Prot. James* 9:2.

2

The Birth of the Savior

Now in Nazareth[1] Mary was keeping busy with household chores and finishing her work on the temple veil. Joseph needed to leave town for a period of time to handle several projects that required his presence, especially in Capernaum. On a day just like any other, in the cool of the morning, Mary took a pitcher and headed to the village spring to fetch some water. No one was on the road. The air was cool, gentle, and quite inviting. Mary was strolling along the rickety stone path, deep in thought. She came to the spring, dipped her pitcher into the water, and began to fill it. At that very moment, a heavenly being[2] spoke to her, saying: "Rejoice, Mary!"

Mary was troubled. She looked to her left, then to her right, but she saw nothing. She did not hear anything else. Even more, there was no one else present; if someone else had been there, she could have asked them if they had just heard the voice too. So, with haste and some trepidation, she took her amphora, fastened it to her right hip, and hurried home. When she got there, she bolted the door shut and said nothing to anyone. Joseph was gone, so she could not ask for his advice, and Simeon was too small. For a moment she thought it could have been some sort of attempt by the devil to deceive her. She prayed to God in her heart: "Give

---

1 So reads the *Gospel of the Birth of Mary.* Other apocryphal texts do not specify the location or place them in Jerusalem (e.g., *Protoevangelium of James* or *Armenian Gospel of the Infancy*).

2 *(Cop.) Gos. Heb.* (Coptic version of Cyril [de Santos, 45]).

ear to your servant, Lord, and do not let her fall into the hands of the wicked destroyer, in one of the tempter's ambushes. In you I hope and trust." And with tears in her eyes, fearful of what had just happened, she continued in her work.[3]

Three days later, while the girl was still busy with the curtain for the sanctuary, an angel appeared in bodily form right before her eyes. The room was flooded with extraordinary brilliance, and the angel greeted her kindly, saying: "Greetings, Mary! Do not be afraid. The Lord is with you and you will be more blessed than all the women and all the men who have ever lived."[4]

The virgin was so accustomed to visiting angels that she was not afraid at all. Not even the great brightness that accompanied the angel caused her to fear. She just went about her business as usual, somewhat surprised by everything the angel had said to her. This visit was an extraordinary one though. Nothing really triggered any extra significance in Mary's mind, mainly because the angel looked exactly as the angels had in the past. But this angel was very different. The divine Word had taken the appearance of Michael, and it was the Word who was speaking directly to Mary this time.[5] The angel-Word knew what the maiden was thinking and spoke immediately to her: "Do not be afraid, Mary, for you have found favor in the sight of God because you have chosen the path of chastity. Therefore, you will conceive and give birth to a son."[6]

Mary then asked him in a very direct way: "So, you are saying I am going to conceive a child, and then give birth just like other women do?" To which the angel answered: "No, Mary. The power of the Lord is going to overshadow you. You will conceive by his Word and the fruit of your womb shall be called the Son of the Most High."[7] "Mary, do not think that you are going to conceive

---

3   (Arm.) Gos. Inf. 5:2.
4   Luke 1:28.
5   Ep. Apost. 14.
6   Gos. Bir. Mary 9:2.
7   Luke 1:31–32.

this child in a human way," the angel continued. "This will all come to pass apart from marital relations, and you will remain a virgin. Your offspring will be conceived and born without sin. You shall name him Jesus, for he will save his people from their sins. You will bring forth a King, whose dominion spans heaven and earth and who reigns from generation to generation."[8]

Then the angel departed from her. Mary heartily accepted the celestial visit, from the moment the Word of God began his descent from the heights of the heaven, through the other heavens, all the way down to where Mary stood. The Word took the form of an angel in order to go unnoticed by the powers that rule in those in-between areas. Michael, Raphael, and Gabriel accompanied him down to the fifth heaven thinking he was an angel. Then they realized who he was and let him go the rest of the way alone.[9] The Divine Word entered Mary by way of her ear, and the girl experienced a rush of sensations in her innermost, like gold being purified in a crucible. Her pregnancy began at that moment, on the fifteenth day of Nisan, which corresponded to April 6th, the fourth day of the week, at the third hour. On earth the same Holy Spirit let her know what had happened inside her body, specifically that she conceived a child, while up in heaven angelic choirs were singing songs of praise to God for this monumental event.[10] During all this, an angel of the Lord appeared in Persia and announced the future birth of the Savior to the three most powerful kings. They were magicians, prophets, and descendants of Balaam the son of Beor,[11] the soothsayer who practiced his art alongside the banks of the Great River Euphrates[12] and had predicted that a star would be born from Jacob.[13] Persia was powerful in the East during that time. There was a dynasty of three brothers that ruled over vast

---

8   *Ps.-Mt.* 9:1–2.
9   *Ep. Apost.* 13.
10   *(Arm.) Gos. Inf.* 5:10.
11   Origen, *Homilies on Numbers* 18:7 and 18:4.
12   Num 22:5.
13   Num 24:17.

territories: Melcon ruled the Persians, Balthazar ruled the Indians, and Gaspar the Arabs. When the angel appeared to them, they were assembled as a family. Afterwards, they started planning their trek to go see the child and worship him.

There were a few moments over the next few days that Mary was attacked with doubt. In those moments of worry, she asked herself: "Why has this happened to me? What am I going to say to convince people who do not believe me? When has anyone seen a woman conceive without being with a man? If I tell them what has happened, they will just laugh at me; but I cannot lie. And if I am branded an adulteress, how can I ever escape that? It is a difficult thing to be punished when you are innocent!"[14]

The days passed slowly as Mary concluded her work on the scarlet veil. Since Joseph was still outside of Nazareth, Mary and two of her servants were in charge of transporting her part of the veil to Jerusalem. Joseph was working around Capernaum, and they decided they would meet in the holy city. The trip to the Jerusalem was uneventful. When Mary arrived, she presented the veil to the high priest. He was greatly pleased to see the wonderful craftsmanship that went into all of the spinning, embroidery, and finesse as a whole.

Although trips were bothersome and cumbersome, even in such a small country, Mary decided to go and visit her cousin Elizabeth, who was finally pregnant after years of hoping and praying to God. Elizabeth had conceived on the twentieth of the month of Teshrin (i.e., October 9th), and the child that would become the forerunner of Jesus was moving about inside her womb. Mary spent three months in the house of Zechariah and Elizabeth.[15] Mary's pregnancy was progressing, and it was becoming noticeable to others. She could no longer hide it with her clothes. Worried about what people might say, she decided to head back home. She made the trip in the same amount of time it took to travel to the capital. Once she arrived in Nazareth, she

---

14   (Arm.) Gos. Inf. 5:11.

15   Luke 1:39ff.

tried not to go out and was hiding from the children of Israel, fearful of whatever insults they might hurl at her. She was sixteen years old when all of this took place.[16]

After six months or so, Joseph concluded his work outside of Nazareth. Mary received him with joy and worry. On the day Joseph returned, she prepared a special meal for him. After setting the table, they sat down, ate, and enjoyed the meal together. Afterwards, Joseph leaned over a small bed that was in the room and looked at Mary. He noted that her face had changed and that she was nervously moving about the room. That prompted him to ask her: "My daughter, what is wrong? I can see that your youthful grace has changed. You seem a little different." Mary answered: "Why are you asking me such questions? What are you trying to say?" Joseph replied: "That is a strange answer. What is wrong? You seem a little sad. I can see it on your face. Has someone said something to hurt you? Are you upset about something?"

Mary did not immediately respond, so Joseph leaned back in the bed. As he looked at his wife, he realized that she was pregnant. At first, he was just thinking maybe it was so, but the more he looked at her the more he was convinced—Mary was definitely pregnant.[17]

Joseph was speechless. He turned away from Mary and went to his room. He was pulling his hair and a thousand questions were running through his mind—a thousand questions, but not one answer. He cursed his old age and the moment that he had accepted this virgin in his home. His head was spinning in circles, trying to think up an explanation and a way that he could escape public ridicule. After all, Mary had only been placed into his care. He could hear them now: "He received the virgin of the temple, and he could not even keep her pure." Needless to say, he struggled on many fronts. He asked the maidens who always accompanied Mary at home if it was possible that she had been involved with a man. The girls responded in the negative. Some of them even told

16   *Prot. James* 12:3.
17   *(Arm.) Gos. Inf.* 6:1.

Joseph how Mary would spend many hours in prayer and how she spoke to angels. They even speculated that the pregnancy could have been due to some angelic intervention. But Joseph replied: "Why are you so set on making me believe that it was an angel who has left her pregnant? Maybe someone pretended to be an angel and has deceived her?" Joseph was hurt, and those thoughts running through his head caused him lots of turmoil and anxiety. He simply did not know what to do. "How can I show my face around the priests?" he asked himself. "What face shall I bring when I come before God? What am I to do?"

Right when it seemed like the best thing, he could do was leave Mary and divorce her in private,[18] an angel of God appeared to him in a dream and explained what was happening. When he awoke, Joseph was quiet and resolved to take Mary as his wife. To avoid any small-town gossip, he decided to move to Jerusalem for a while. And so they did.[19]

Little by little the rumor that Mary was pregnant spread around the city. A malicious individual who called himself a friend of the family broke the news to the priest. Here is what happened. Joseph always used to go to the synagogue. After the services he liked to chat with friends and acquaintances. But during this whole ordeal, starting around the time they had taken the trip and the whole situation was still unclear, he stopped doing so. He did not even dare to appear in public. Then, Annas the scribe visited him at his home, and during the conversation asked him: "Why have you not come to the services at the synagogue?" Joseph said: "I was just so tired from my trip, and I devoted some time when I got home to just rest."

But while Annas was visiting Joseph in his home, he realized that Mary was pregnant. He got so excited that he almost left without even saying goodbye. He jumped up, said his farewells as quickly as he could, and he went straight to the priest to report the

---

18   Matt 1:19.

19   This is found both in the *Armenian Gospel of the Infancy* and the *Protoevangelium of James*.

news. Annas said to the priest: "That Joseph has committed a serious crime." The priest replied: "What are you talking about?" Annas responded: "Joseph raped that girl who was placed into his care. And if you do not believe me, send some people to check it out."[20]

So, the temple servants went to Joseph's house. When they saw that Mary was pregnant, they grabbed Joseph and took him to the temple. The pontiff was livid. He began to mock the old man for the fraud he had supposedly committed. But Joseph swore that he did not touch the girl and that the pregnancy was something divine. Nobody believed him. The pontiff said to the bystanders: "As sure as God lives, I will make you drink the water of the Lord and instantly your sin will be revealed."

This was a custom that they had back then. The "water of the Lord" referred to the water that flowed ever so slightly from a turbulent spring near the temple. No one dared to drink from it. Tradition was that the waters were poisoned. It was only to be used in situations like this one, to determine a person's innocence or guilt. This water was given to those who were accused of certain crimes that could not easily be tried—especially, for example, women who were accused of committing adultery by their jealous husbands.[21] Such individuals had to drink this bitter and deadly water, according to tradition. The priest would add some of the dust collected from the innermost parts of the sanctuary. The defendant who drank this water and felt nothing in his or her stomach region was cleared of all accusations. But if that person was guilty, it is said that God would use the water like poison and would cause a deadly disease to ensue.

Because this was Joseph and Mary, a whole host of people gathered on the temple mount—so many it was impossible to count them. The servants of the priests also took Mary into the sanctuary. The people were saying to her: "Confess your sin at once and save yourself from the test." But the girl said not a word. Joseph was called before the altar and was given the bitter and deadly

20   *Prot. James* 15.
21   Num 5:12ff.

water to drink. He drank the water with absolute confidence. He had to walk around the altar seven times, and then he was sent out to the desert near Jerusalem. But after a while, the old man returned safely to the temple. The priest did the same thing with Mary. Her demeanor, which projected hope, almost made the test unnecessary. Still, her claims of innocence were subject to the test. The young girl took the jug of water into her shaky hands. They were shaking because there were so many people watching her, and it felt like all of them thought she was guilty. The people looked on, as she remained quiet. They thought her silence and anxiety were a sign of her guilt. Mary drank the water, walked around the altar seven times, and was sent out to the desert. After a while, long enough to cause people to worry, Mary returned safe and sound.[22] At that moment an almost universal cry for joy erupted, though some of the people were still confused. After all, how could it be? She was pregnant, but yet the test had proven her innocence. That led to a whole flurry of opinions. Some called her a saint and viewed everything as a miracle; others returned to their homes doubtful of her innocence. Even though there were many examples of something like this—women conceiving a child by divine action— particularly among the Gentiles (e.g., by Apollo; by Zeus), they could not make sense of it all. At the moment, everything was on hold pending further developments.[23] And the priest offered his official proclamation, saying: "Since God has not condemned you, neither shall we; go in peace."

The pregnancy ran its normal course[24] and it came time for Mary to give birth. It was during that time that an edict was issued by Caesar Augustus requiring everyone in the Empire to return to his or her place of birth.[25] The edict called for a census throughout the Empire so that they could more precisely tax everyone's wealth and property, which included the male and female servants of

---

22   *Prot. James* 16.

23   *Ps.-Mt.* 12:4.

24   *Ascen. Isa.* 11:6, 7, 13: The pregnancy lasted only two months.

25   Luke 2:1.

each family.[26] And so Joseph was forced to travel to Bethlehem along with his wife, who was also a descendent of Judah, from the house and lineage of David.[27] Joseph no longer had any business in Bethlehem, not even a home. They left everything when they moved to Nazareth. But given its close proximity, he hoped to take care of everything quickly so that he could return immediately to Jerusalem. He prepared a mule and put Mary on it. Joseph took the bridle and led the beast by foot. As they journeyed, the old man watched Mary and could see that she had a somewhat sad face. He thought to himself: "She is probably uncomfortable riding on the mule while she is pregnant." He looked at her again, and it made Mary happy. At one point she told Joseph: "I feel sad and happy at the same time. I see two people in front of me . . . one who weeps and one who rejoices." Joseph said: "Hold on tight, and lean on the mule. This is no time to speak useless words."

At that moment a beautiful child, wearing a splendid garment, appeared to Mary and Joseph. He spoke to Joseph: "Why did you say they were useless words? Mary spoke of two peoples. She has seen the Jews who mourn because they depart from their God, and she has seen the Gentiles who rejoice because they will be converted to the Lord, in accordance with the promises he made to our fathers."[28] And after these words were spoken, the time for Mary to give birth had arrived. Mary said: "Joseph, put me down because the fruit of my womb is pushing to come out." The old man helped her off the mule, thinking to himself: "Where can I take her to protect her modesty? I mean we are in field! Where can we go?"

They wandered past a place where they found a cave next to the road. It just so happened to be near the tomb of Rachel, the wife of Jacob, mother of Joseph and Benjamin, two of the patriarchs. The land was holy.[29] The cave had a narrow entrance, but then it opened up and went down. If they were going to use this

26   (Arm.) Gos. Inf. 8:1; B. Inf. Sav. 59.

27   Ps.-Mt. 13:1.

28   Ps.-Mt. 13:1.

29   Hist. Jos. Carp. 7:2.

cave, they needed to go down to the part that was underground. Because of that, there was not a lot of light. But right when Mary entered the cave the site was flooded with brightness, and everything was glowing as if the sun itself was inside the cave. That divine light illuminated the cave like it lights up the earth at noon on a cloudless day.[30]

Joseph left Mary with Simeon once he made sure she was comfortable. He left the cave and went to the city of Bethlehem in search of a midwife. He was making pretty good time at first, but suddenly he felt like he could no longer walk. He lifted his eyes up to the sky and it seemed for moment as if the air was shaking with wonder. He turned his head and looked around the sky. Everything was standing still, and birds up there in the sky frozen in time. Joseph, completely blown away, turned his gaze to the ground. The winds had died down and the leaves of the trees had no movement. In the distance he saw some laborers in the act of eating next to a container, with their hands around it. But those who looked like they were chewing were not actually chewing; those who looked like they were taking the food out of the container did not budge; those who looked like they were lifting some food to their mouths never let it touch their lips. Everything was frozen. Everyone was frozen. There were some sheep that were being herded by a shepherd boy, but he did not move an inch. He was perfectly still. The shepherd who raised his staff with his right hand kept it frozen in the air. Even the river stopped flowing. Some kids that were sipping water from its banks did not lift their heads. Their lips just stayed kissing the water. Joseph did not know why, but the course of nature had broken all the rules.[31] This occurred five thousand years after the creation of the world,[32] on the twentieth of May.[33] This is all we have in our documents about the birth of Jesus. It seems as if the

---

30   *Ps.-Mt.* 13:2; *B. Inf. Sav.* 65.

31   *Prot. James* 18:2; *B. Inf. Sav.* 72.

32   *Desc. Chr. ad. Inf.* 3; *L.A.E.* 42.

33   Cf. the views of Clement of Alexandria, *Stromata* 1:21:145.

circumstances surrounding Jesus' birth had stopped up the pen of the authors. As Homer did not dare at any time to describe the wonderful beauty of Helena for fear of not doing justice to her beauty with mere words, none of the authors of the relevant texts dared to attempt any description of the birth of the hero of this story but left the momentous details all veiled in silence.

For Joseph it felt like this remarkable phenomenon of universal pause had lasted only a moment. After that time, the patriarch was able to continue his search. But behold, the old man saw a girl in the near distance coming down a path headed directly towards him. In one hand she was carrying some linens and in the other a kind of stool, like the one midwife in Israel would sit on when assisting a woman in giving birth. Immediately, Joseph knew she was a midwife. He asked her: "Daughter, where are you going with that stool?" She answered: "I was sent here by my teacher. A young girl appeared in our home with haste, and she showed us how we could assist with a new birth, by a girl who is giving birth for the first time. My madam, Zelomi,[34] sent me ahead of her because she is older. She is coming though. The truth is that I did not know where the cave was located. I asked some people, and they did not know anything about it either."[35]

Indeed, a little while later the old woman appeared. Joseph urged her to hurry to the cave. The old woman said to Joseph: "I am old and weak, and my apprentice lacks experience. Therefore, I also called upon another midwife to help us. I hope she comes soon." So, they headed to the cave together. Zelomi was interested in Mary and asked Joseph many questions. Joseph was not very interested in answering her though. The midwife asked: "She is not your wife yet." He answered: "No. This is Mary, the one who was raised in the temple. She has conceived this child in a supernatural

34   (Arm.) Gos. Inf. 8:9: According to this text, the midwife is actually Eve, the mother of all the living, who witnesses from heaven the great event taking place; the second Eve, Mary, will give birth to a child that will restore everything she destroyed in paradise.

35   Hist. Jos. Carp. 14 (see Bauer, Das Leben Jesu, 62).

way." "How can this be?," the midwife asked. Joseph answered: "Well, come and see." And Joseph did not utter another word.[36]

Finally, they entered the cave. The old man said: "Please, go and care for Mary." The midwife was overwhelmed with fear when she entered because she saw the bright and mysterious light that illumined the cave. The sun was setting, so she expected it to be super dark inside.[37] The midwife entered and stood before Mary. Mary had already given birth all by herself,[38] and she was sitting on a round stone with a beautiful child in her arms. She had given birth to her child away from the men and without any help. Mary smiled, while Joseph and Zelomi had a stunned look across their faces. The old man said to Mary: "I brought this woman to you . . . just in case you needed some medical attention."

The midwife examined the child and his mother for a period of time, while Joseph and Simeon respectfully kept their distance. Suddenly, Zelomi cried out with a loud voice that rang throughout every corner of the cave. Simeon began to shake and shouted to the midwife: "Ma'am, is everything okay? Is she still alive?" The midwife did not respond, but between shouts and gasps she offered these clear words: "What mercy, my Lord and great God, because never has anyone seen what I seen now! The mother's breasts are swollen with milk and, simultaneously, a newborn child is denouncing the virginity of his mother![39] There is no stain of blood on the newborn, no pain, no afterbirth.[40] This is wonderful! No wonder the light in this cave has multiplied its

---

36   *Prot. James* 19; *B. Inf. Sav.* 68.

37   *(Arab.) Gos. Inf.* 3:1.

38   *B. Inf. Sav.* 73.

39   *Gos. Phil.* 17 (81–83, 91) denies the virginity of Mary. Jesus is born as all children are, the natural son of Joseph and Mary. From his baptism in the Jordan the heavenly Christ descends upon Jesus and unites the two, physical body and divine person, into a direct son of God the Father and of the "Virgin," his eternal spouse (called "Thinking," "Silence," etc.).

40   *Ps.-Mt.* 13:3. Cf. *Ascen. Isa.* 11:4, and *Acts Pet.* 24: birth without midwife, wonderful, painless, while the people of Bethlehem did not believe that Mary had given birth.

brightness and darkens even the sun with its glare. What intense and sweet clarity, what perfume and sweet aroma. This light has come to us as the dew comes down from heaven to the meadows. Its aroma is more potent than the perfume of all the ointments of the earth."[41]

Zelomi remained in the cave a good while longer. She took the child in her arms and saw that he did not weigh like other newborns do; he was much lighter and brighter in appearance. She was surprised because the child did not cry like other children either. The midwife looked at him intently, and the newborn gave her a very pleasant smile; and he looked at her with a penetrating gaze, totally unusual for a child this age. His face changed from friendly to stern, yet still very soft and human.[42]

Finally, Zelomi prepared to leave the cave. At that moment, the younger midwife, named Salome arrived. Zelomi shouted with joy: "Salome, Salome, the most wonderful thing ever has just happened. A virgin has given birth! The world has never seen anything like this." But Salome just sort of smirked, a sign of her unbelief, and mocked Zelomi's words. Salome said: "As sure as the Lord lives, I will not believe such a thing unless I first insert my finger and test her condition for myself."

Salome went into the cave immediately. The brightness of the light inside the cave seemed more bearable at that time. The young midwife had barely noticed the child or taken notice of the interior of the cave before she said to Mary: "If you are willing, I would like to examine you. There is quite a story being told about your condition." Salome, then, inserted her finger into Mary and felt her hymen. And immediately she let out a horrible scream and cried out: "Woe is me! My iniquity and my disbelief are to blame! Because I tested the living God, my hand is now burnt to a crisp!"

Everyone was scared to death at what they saw. Salome was moaning and crying out to God, full of contrition, pleading in her defense about all the good things that had been accomplished

---

41   *B. Inf. Sav.* 73.
42   *B. Inf. Sav.* 84.

among the children of Israel by people in her trade. That lasted a short amount of time. The cave would have been deafening silent were it not for the intense moans of Salome. Suddenly, an angel from heaven appeared and told the midwife: "Salome, Salome, the Lord has heard you and accepted your repentance. Reach out your hand to the child, pick him up, and you shall have joy and gladness."

The woman did as the angel said. She took Jesus into her arms, difficult as that was to do, and she was immediately healed. Her hand, which was dried, charred black from being burnt and on the brink of needing amputation, began to heal. After just a few moments it was completely healed with rosy, smooth, and beautiful skin. She stayed there in the cave a while and, afterwards, departed, ready to tell everyone about everything she had seen and heard. Before she could even cross the threshold, she heard a voice from heaven, saying: "Salome, do not tell of the wonders you have seen here until the child is in Jerusalem."[43]

The newborn was behaving normally. He soon took to his mother's breast and fed himself with joy from the milk that flowed in abundance. Mary, despite being a virgin, produced a generous amount of milk for the child.

Salome did not do as the voice from heaven commanded. Instead, she went out and told anyone and everyone all about the wonders she had witnessed in the cave.[44] Some local shepherds also claimed to have seen some wonders. "The night was still," they said, "and we were sitting in the field keeping watch. The moon had risen into the sky, full of splendor, and its light outlined the shapes of the surrounding cliffs. At midnight, we heard some choirs of angels singing hymns and blessing us with their praises to God."[45]

As if these rare phenomena were not enough, a new shining star appeared in the sky. It was way, way up in the sky, but it

---

43   *Prot. James* 20.

44   *Ps.-Mt.* 13:5.

45   *B. Inf. Sav.* 82.

seemed as if its light emanated down towards the cave. The locals claimed that they had never seen anything like it before. Some spiritual men from Jerusalem with the gift of prophecy wondered whether it might not be the sign of the birth of the Messiah. All the promises made by God to Israel had to be fulfilled. It was not long before the shepherds made their way to the cave carrying some gifts, fresh milk, and cheese.[46] With Joseph's permission, they entered the cave. They worshiped the child and offered their greetings to the mother. They had lit a fire outside, so after a little while they went outside and just began to rejoice. At the same time, they could see the heavenly hosts up above praising God. It was as if the cave had turned into the temple of a sublime world, one where the languages of heaven and earth converged in ringing out glory to God for the miraculous birth of the child inside the cave.[47]

The cave was pretty uncomfortable in almost every respect. So, a few days after the child's birth, Joseph went looking for a more suitable place. He tried to get a place in Bethlehem's only inn, but a few caravans had already arrived and their camels and goods left no vacancy. There was not even room for them in the courtyard.[48] Still, Joseph did not want to set out on any trip just yet, short as it was, because Mary had just given birth. So, he continued his search for other accommodations. Near the cave there was an abandoned farmhouse with a stable. For Joseph it seemed like this place was, for lack of other accommodations, much better than the cave. And so it happened that a few days following the birth of Jesus, Mary moved from the cave to the stable where there was a manger for the horses. She wrapped the child in some swaddling clothes and placed him on some hay. Simeon and Joseph were there as well. The mule that carried them, together with an ox—it is not known from where that animal came—stayed by the child's side continually, worshiping him

46   B. Inf. Sav. 85.
47   (Arab.) Gos. Inf. 4:1.
48   Luke 2:7.

and keeping him warm with their breath. This fulfilled what the prophet Isaiah announced: "An ox knows its owner, and a donkey its master's manger."[49] Joseph went out everyday and sought sustenance in the surrounding farms. Everyone provided for their needs without Joseph having to bother anyone or even utter a word, because that is the way God wanted it.[50] Joseph, who had remarkable foresight, had carried with him enough coins in his bag so that they lacked nothing.

They arrived back in Bethlehem six days after Jesus was born. They rested a little while and then continued on their way to Jerusalem. On the eighth day Jesus was circumcised.[51] A wise lawyer named Joel was responsible for the small surgery; but even when he touched the iron to the newborn's delicate skin, producing only a few drops of blood, there was no scar. The child was named Jesus as the angel commanded.[52] Mary observed the quarantine period prescribed by the Mosaic Law for purification, although not strictly required to do so based on what we know from Salome's observation. Once that period was finished, the child was presented in the temple.[53] This is when the events with Simeon and the prophetess Anna took place.[54] Afterwards they returned to Bethlehem, staying temporarily in the barn that Joseph found near the cave.

---

49   Isa 1:3.

50   *(Arm.) Gos. Inf.* 12:1.

51   *(Arab.) Gos. Inf.* 5:1: The circumcision took place in the same cave by the hand of the same midwife. She saved the foreskin in a jar of nard and her daughter carefully kept it. This is the bottle of perfume that was eventually purchased by Mary, the sinner, and poured upon the head and feet of Jesus.

52   Luke 1:31.

53   *(Arm.) Gos. Inf.* 12: The circumcision and the presentation in the temple take place after the visit of the Magi.

54   *Ps.-Mt.* 15; *(Arab.) Gos. Inf.* 6; Luke 2:25–38.

Herod the King

The family spent a period of time in a quiet little farmhouse, not far outside Bethlehem.[1] One day a huge procession came to Jerusalem: three kings from the East,[2] with a large entourage of twelve thousand men, four thousand with each king.[3] Their presence, as one can imagine, grabbed the attention of the whole city. We already know about how an angel of God was responsible for announcing the news of the virginal conception in the East, and also how these kings immediately prepared for the journey. They soon set out and were guided by the star that had appeared mysteriously in the sky. That star disappeared somewhere on the outskirts of Jerusalem. It is true that not everyone could see the star, which was actually an angel who had temporarily assumed the appearance of a star.[4] That star was brighter than all the other heavenly bodies. At times it seemed as if the sun, moon, and other stars encircled it to form a respectful chorus. And this star, positioned in the center, far surpassed the others in splendor.[5]

Obviously, the procession did not go unnoticed by King Herod's spies, which were distributed all throughout the region. The three important figures that arrived—some said they were magicians, others that they were priest-kings from the Persian

---

1   *Ps.-Mt.* 16:1 says it was two years.

2   Matt 2:1ff.

3   *(Arm.) Gos. Inf.* 11:1.

4   *(Arab.) Gos. Inf.* 7:1.

5   Ignatius of Antioch, *Epistle to the Ephesians* 19:2.

regions—were resolved in their search for the newborn King of the Jews. Such a dangerous matter reached the ears of the king, who, being deeply disturbed, immediately summoned them to his palace. Anyone who knew anything about the past few years would know nothing good was on the horizon. Dozens of people who opposed the king had already been put to death, including his own sons, who had conspired against him, as well as some of his ten wives. Shortly before the magi arrived, the city of Sebaste, which is located in Samaria, had witnessed the hanging of two of the monarch's other children (conspiring with Mariamme) for plotting a revolution against their father. The king was informed of a prophecy of Zaradust,[6] which spoke of a virgin who would give birth to a son, who would be sacrificed by the Jews and afterwards ascend to heaven. Upon hearing such news and given such a large number of visitors, Herod placed his garrison on alert.

The three kings were presented to the Jewish monarch after being introduced by some ambassadors.[7] They all exchanged gifts and then asked each other some questions. The magi-kings told Herod about their search for the newborn king of the Jews, and they told him about how a prophecy was written down and had been preserved in Persia, handed down from generation to generation, until an angel announced its fulfillment to them. They included how that prophecy had its origin in Seth, the son of Adam, who had received it from his father. Paradise was located in Persia, so it was fitting for its inhabitants to care for this prophecy. Seth, before he died, entrusted the prophecy to his children all the way to Noah. And so did Noah after the Flood, to Abraham, Melchizedek, all the way to Cyrus, the king of Persia.

Herod stared at the magi, his eyes like knives, very concerned at all he was hearing. At one point he wanted to seize the visitors, but, when he went to give the order, an earthquake hit and shook the palace. Then, when everything calmed down, his son Archelaus jumped in, pleading out of fear for no one to do anything to the

---

6   (Arab.) Gos. Inf. 7:1 = Zoroaster.

7   (Arm.) Gos. Inf. 11:6.

visitors. He pretended to rejoice at the news and even offered some additional gifts to carry on the journey for the news. Herod told them that, according to the Jewish Scriptures, the birthplace of the newborn king could be none other than Bethlehem, the City of David.[8] Afterwards, he dismissed the magi with his pretend blessings and treacherous smile.[9]

The star, which was momentarily hidden to prevent those in Jerusalem from seeing it, reappeared and led the entire procession to Bethlehem. Joseph, who happened to be outside, saw the magi as they approached. He spoke to Simeon his companion: "Why do you think this procession is coming to meet us? They look like they have traveled a long way. I shall go out to meet them."

He took a few steps before stopping out of fear once he saw how many of the men were armed. He spoke again to Simeon: "I think they are some sort of prophets because they are of observing everything and discussing it among themselves. They do not look like they are from around here judging by their clothes. I will get a little closer." He approached them and asked: "What are you looking for, strangers?" They barely said anything, only saying that a special guide—an angel—had led them to the location. They said: "We have been following a star to this place so that we can see the king of the Jews." Joseph replied: "You should probably head to Jerusalem then, because that is where you will find the temple of the Lord."

Joseph knew of the greatness of the child, but he could not imagine that he was the "king of the Jews." He certainly could not imagine that some Persians would have traveled so far to worship him. The three kings told Joseph all about their meeting with Herod and how the king had even sent his own gifts for the child. He had all but offered the crown that he wore with a white turban upon his head. Joseph gave them permission and the three kings came at last to where the manger was, leaving their entourage outside. They stayed a long time, talking to Mary and contemplating the

---

8   Matt 2:6.

9   *(Arm.) Gos. Inf.* 11:12–14.

child, whom they worshiped by prostrating themselves on the ground. Joseph kept his distance, watching curiously and not uttering a word. And Simeon got lost in all the details. The three magi, after worshiping and kissing the child on his feet, presented him with many gifts, including gold, frankincense, and myrrh.[10] The myrrh signified that the infant would later die for humanity and that he would be buried, the gold characterized him as king, and the incense as God.[11] These gifts were very old. Adam had collected some of them after the fall, anticipating (by way of divine illumination) the birth of the one who would become the "second Adam." He placed them in a cave where he kept all of his treasures. Past generations, in accordance with the instructions given by Adam to his son Seth, preserved these gifts in Persia. And the magi had now brought them to Bethlehem.[12] All Mary could offer them in return was but one of the child's cloths that she had wrapped Jesus in. The magi agreed, and they took it with joy as one of their most precious possessions. To Joseph they said: "O blessed man. Soon you shall know exactly who this child is that you protect. His name is greater than yours and the reason that you can even call yourself his father is based on the fact that you serve him. He will save the peoples for his own name's sake, shall break the sting of death, and destroy the power of hell. Kings will serve him and the tribes of the earth will worship him." Joseph was shocked, asking: "How do you know all of this?" They answered: "We too have our own Scriptures that speak of him. Moreover, we have seen his star, which is our divine messenger."

After their long visit, the kings decided they would return to Jerusalem so that they could inform Herod of all that had transpired. But it was late, too late to set out, so they decided to rest there and depart the next morning. They ordered their people to set up camp there in Bethlehem. They did as they were directed. That night an

10   *B. Inf. Sav.* 89–92.

11   Irenaeus, *Against Heresies* 3:9:2; Origen, *Against Celsus* 1:60.

12   *Cave of Treasures*, in C. Bezold, *Die Schatzhöhle*, 56ff.; there is an allusion to this in the Acts of Pilate (*Desc. Chr. ad. Inf.* 3).

angel of God appeared to them in a dream.[13] The angel ordered them to return directly to Persia by way of a different route, in order to circumvent Herod's evil plans to destroy the child. The kings joyfully did exactly as the angel commanded. Upon reaching their land in Persia, their barons and princes questioned them, and the kings reported all that had happened. Then they then lit a fire, as was their custom, and worshiped it. According to their religion, the fire represented the divine. They thought the best way they could honor the child was to offer the cloth that had touched the body of Jesus into the fire. They figured it would be consumed by the fire and go up in smoke to heaven. And so they did, only the cloth was not consumed. The fire flickered a little, but continued to burn until it finally just went out. The cloth was found among the ashes completely intact, as if the flames had not touched it at all. The magi kept the cloth among their treasures.[14]

After some time passed, King Herod began to think that the magi were taking forever to return and give him a report. He sent for a certain individual in Bethlehem named Begor, who was one of the king's spies. Begor reported in great detail all that had transpired in Bethlehem—the worship of the child, the present Mary had given the magi, and how they had returned to Persia via a different route. Herod was absolutely livid. Motivated by his anger, he called for all of his advisers and courtiers to assemble, and he sought their counsel. Most agreed that he should not worry. Many, they argued, had arisen in Israel, pretending to be someone important—a king or messiah—only for their deeds, after only a few days or months, to prove insignificant and their memory fade into obscurity. Others advised him more or less the same thing, arguing that several days had passed and the infant, along with his parents, would have already fled to a faraway place, safe from the king's reach.

Herod dismissed all of his advisers and contemplated their counsel. In the end, he decided not to run the risk. His reign had

---

13 *Prot. James* 21:4; *Ps.-Mt.* 16:2.

14 *(Arab.) Gos. Inf.* 8.

been threatened in many ways before, but all who dared had paid with their lives for plotting against the crown. He was on guard at all times. And since he was now at the end of his life, he wanted to live more peacefully, if at all possible. So, he decided to take a drastic decision. Spies had informed him that the child was still in Bethlehem, but his parents had changed where they were staying a few times. He called the head of his personal guard and the two of them hatched a secret plan. Not even his advisers were privy to it. The plan was to quash this new threat to the throne by having all of the children in Bethlehem under the age of two years put to death.[15] They planned to kill all of them in a single day, using the same number of soldiers as there were children in the town so that none could escape. The chief guard brought his best men for the job and promised them a good reward if they succeeded in the operation. The king's compensation would certainly be more than enough.

The day before this terrible misfortune took place, when Jesus was already about a year old, Joseph received another message from God while he was sleeping telling him to immediately depart from Bethlehem and head to Egypt. Immediately, the patriarch started gathering up all of their belongings, which were very few. They quietly hit the road the next morning, heading south towards Hebron.[16] Three young men, who Joseph had hired as servants, and a girl, hired to help with Mary, accompanied them on the journey.[17] After a while, they turned west towards the coast and the city of Gaza. Joseph was hoping to settle somewhere in the Egyptian delta, since many Jews lived there that could help him during their trial. Not even twenty-four hours had passed since they left, and the king's soldiers, right at the break of dawn, started to slaughter the children in Bethlehem. A total of 360 children were slain.[18] People were terrified; their pain and anger

---

15   Matt 2:13–23.

16   (Arm.) Gos. Inf. 15:2.

17   Ps.-Mt. 18:1.

18   (Arm.) Gos. Inf. 13:5.

were boiling, but nobody dared to lift a finger, knowing how cruel Herod could be and fearing he might react by doing something even more terrible.

The king was not satisfied with the results, so he ordered the murder of Jesus' relatives, even though they were not even in Bethlehem. He was certain that Zechariah the priest and his wife were related to Mary, so he ordered the murder of John, who was Jesus' cousin. An angel alerted Elizabeth to the news that soldiers of the king were on their way to kill her son. She took him in her arms and fled straight to the mountains, not telling anyone, not even her husband, about their sudden flight because she did not want to compromise their safety; in the meantime, Zechariah continued his work in the temple. Amid the crags Elizabeth started looking for a suitable place to hide, but she just could not find a safe place. Crying out, she said: "My God, save me from Herod and his armies! You are my mountain, O God. Have mercy on me and hide me and this child in your loving arms!" Immediately, the mountainside opened, and they entered the rocks. They found themselves in a dark and mysterious cave. Though they had no light, the cave was illumined. And they were accompanied by an angel of God, who gave them food, light, and protection.[19]

Traveling to the mountains would have been fatal to Zechariah, the father of John. As a priest he would not have wanted to leave the temple, and, knowing the possibility of retaliation, he continued his service therein. Herod's henchmen showed up at the holy place early in the morning and asked Zechariah: "Where have you hidden your son?" He replied: "I am here serving God, and I am usually here in the sanctuary all day long. I do not know where my son is."

Herod's men immediately went and reported to him what Zechariah had said. The king was furious. He thought to himself: "Maybe all of this about the newborn baby of Bethlehem is just a hoax. Perhaps Zechariah's son is really this supposed future king of Israel." So, he sent messengers to the temple question him, saying:

19 *Prot. James* 22:2–4.

"Tell us the truth about your son. You know very well that your life is in the king's hands." But Zechariah said nothing and only declared that he was ready to face the consequences. By dawn the assassins of the king were tired of his stubborn silence. Zechariah was slain near the entrance of the sanctuary, in a chamber room that was not very far from the altar. His blood flowed out of his body and was soaked up by the slab floor where his body fell.

A few hours later the rest of the priests gathered for the morning greeting and prayer. But Zechariah did not show up to greet everyone as he usually did. At first they thought he might be praying in the temple, but soon they began to worry and went looking for him. One of them entered a room and saw the blood on the ground. Looking a little further into the room, he saw Zechariah's body lying there. Right then he heard a voice from heaven, saying: "Zechariah has been slain and his blood will not be wiped up until the avenger appears." The priest got out of there as fast as he could. His whole demeanor changed. When he got back to where the other priests were, he struggled to even get the words out as he told them all that he had seen and heard. Everyone took off running to the room where Zechariah's body lay, and with great trepidation they entered the chamber room. The ceiling of the temple let out a terrible creak; it sounded as if the roof was going to collapse and crush everyone underneath. The priests were overcome with fear. They tore their garments in mourning, picked up the body of Zechariah, and prepared it for burial. The news spread quickly outside the temple. The people of Israel were deeply saddened by the cruelty of their king, and they mourned the loss of Zechariah for three days and three nights.[20]

Joseph, Mary, and the child had departed the city of Gaza, which was a long ways from Jerusalem by about forty Roman miles. From there the way to the delta was long. There were no prominent cities along the way where they could stop and rest.

---

20   *Prot. James* 22–24. The aprocryphal Gospel *Genna Marias* (*The Descent of Mary*) attributes the death of Zechariah to the same Jews, who were enraged that the priest reproached them for their corrupted religion (de Santos, 66).

Because of that, they needed to gather supplies to carry with them for the whole journey. After they left the last Jewish city, they came upon a cave and wanted to stop. Mary got off the mule that was carrying her and entered the cave. She sat down and placed Jesus on her lap. There were some dragons in the back of the cave, and they were hissing with horror. Their appearance was terrifying. Their mouths were open and that sight alone was enough to frighten anyone. Joseph, Mary, and the young men who accompanied them were shaking with fear. Jesus then got down from his mother's lap and stood on his own two feet, placing himself right in front of the dragons. They backed up and prostrated themselves before Jesus before quietly returning to their lairs in the darkest recesses of the cave. Mary and Joseph were petrified, but Jesus was perfectly calm and ordered the dragons not to harm anyone from that point forward.[21]

After that terrifying experience, they continued on their journey through the desert toward the first city between Egypt and Judea. Along the way, lions and leopards accompanied them, shepherding them through a region void of roads or people. Jesus showed his parents that they did not need to be afraid of these animals. The beasts walked meekly beside Mary as she rode on her donkey and carried their luggage for them. Joseph had arranged a large chariot drawn by two oxen, which did not show the slightest bit of fear near their ferocious butchers. The presence of Jesus turned them into pets. This reminded Mary of the words of the prophet, which read: "Wolf and the lamb will graze together, and the lion will eat straw like the ox."[22]

By the third day of the journey, the climate started taking its toll on Mary. The air was unbearably dry, the sun was scorching hot, and the lack of a breeze made it all seem even hotter. Mary, seeing a palm tree near the path, said to Joseph: "I need to rest under the shade of that palm tree." Joseph tied the rope around the tree and lowered Mary from the donkey. The mother of Jesus was

---

21   *Ps.-Mt.* 18.
22   Isa 65:25.

hungry and thirsty. She looked at the top of the palm and could see all the delicious fruits hanging from its limbs. "If possible," she said to her husband, "can you get me some of those dates?" Joseph replied: "They are pretty high up. I do not think I can reach them. I am pretty worried at how much water we have too. We are getting pretty low."

Then Jesus, who was sitting peacefully in his mother's lap, said to the palm tree: "Bow down, tree, and give my mother some of your fruit." And at his words the palm tree leaned over so that Mary could pluck some of its fruit. She took the fruit and also gave some to Joseph and the child. And the tree remained leaning over until Jesus ordered it to arise. The child spoke: "We need the water flowing through your roots. Offer it to us so that we can be replenished and fill our containers." Immediately, a spring of very fresh and crystal-clear water sprung up from the ground. They all quenched their thirst and gave water to the animals. They also filled their containers. They spent the night under this palm tree, protected from the elements by its branches. The next day, before they departed, Jesus spoke to the tree: "This privilege I grant you, palm tree: One of your branches shall be transported to and planted by my angels in the paradise of my Father. From now on, you will be the sign of victory, so that everyone who reaches the goal shall receive the palm of victory." At that moment an angel appeared, visible to everyone, and broke away a beautiful palm branch and carried it through the air to paradise. All of them fell to the ground as though dead. Jesus reassured them with these words: "Do not be afraid. This palm branch that has been transferred to Eden shall be a reminder for you of the victory that awaits you."

And so they continued their journey. They all walked along the shore to avoid the heat; though no one knew it, Jesus was actually doing something miraculous, shortening the distance that they were traveling so the journey would not be so hard on his parents and travel companions. This route would normally span a total of fifteen days, but it was shortened to a single day. Towards the end of the day, the travelers were already starting to make out the mountains and cities of Egypt on the horizon in front of them. It was not long before they arrived on the outskirts of Hermopolis. Because they did not know anyone in the city, they sought shelter in a nearby temple, believing that the temple would be safe from bandits.[23]

There was a priest serving in the temple who was responsible for speaking to the people as if Satan was speaking through his mouth. The idols in the temple are basically just a species of the thief Satanael,[24] or Satan, who is given the title and honor of divinity and deceives people into worshiping demons instead of God. That is what idols are—demons.[25] This priest had a three-year-old son, who was possessed by numerous demons. When they overtook him in a demonic fit, the priest's son would rip his garments and throw stones at those who visited the temple. When Joseph's group approached the temple and pitched his tent near the idolatrous shrine, there was a great earthquake. The temple grounds shook, the walls of the temple cracked, and the great idol inside began to jump up and down. Other idols in the altars began moving as well until they fell to the ground all at once and broke into a million pieces. And as they fell, a great clamor was heard, but it was not human. The idols themselves were screaming out for Jesus' death, outraged by how they had been treated.[26] The priest and the people gathered around the temple with curiosity and awe, wondering what in the world had happened and why.

At that exact moment, the son of the priest fell prey to the demons, and he began to wander erratically in the area. Spinning around, he happened to end up where Joseph and his family were. Mary had just finished washing Jesus' cloths and hung them up

---

23   *Ps.-Thom.* 18–22.

24   *Gos. Bart.* 4:25: "In the beginning I was called Satanael, which means "messenger of God," but when I refused to worship the image of God (i.e., recently created man) my name was changed to Satan, which means "angel who guards hell (Tartarus)."

25   *(Arm.) Gos. Inf.* 15:18.

26   *(Arm.) Gos. Inf.* 15:17.

on a piece of wood. The demon-possessed boy was foaming at the
mouth. He turned and violently took one of those cloths and put
it over his head. The demons began to depart from the boy by way
of his mouth in the form of crows and snakes. And immediately
the boy was healed. The priest, the father of the boy, had set out to
find his son. When he found him, the boy was calm, sitting on the
floor, and very peaceful. His father asked: "Son, what happened?"
The child told him everything. The priest was overjoyed, and he
supposed that the foreign family had some god or powerful force
that brought about these strange events. He praised the divinity
while sharing with Joseph and Mary the strange things that had
happened inside the temple and how all the idols had shaken and
were smashed on the ground. Such news did not please the parents
of Jesus. They became nervous, thinking to themselves: "When
we were in the land of Israel, Herod tried to kill the child and
massacred the children in Bethlehem. Now there is no doubt—
when the Egyptians hear what has happened to their idols, they
will have it out for us too. Surely, they will burn us alive."[27]

Soon after, Afrodisius, the governor of the region, showed up
with all of his men. They were heavily armed, having learned of
what had happened in the temple. The priest and Joseph assumed
that the soldiers were there to take revenge against the ones who
had brought about the downfall of idols. But when Afrodisius
surveyed what took place and saw Joseph with his family, he had a
strange sense of fear and respect. He approached them and bowed
down. Then, turning to his men, he said: "If they have caused the
downfall of the idols, we will not lift a finger against them because
their power must be greater than the gods of the temple. They are
Jews, and I read how in the past a pharaoh of this land was once
buried at sea—he along with his whole army—for not heeding
the warning signs God had given them." He said nothing else and
withdrew, leaving them alone.[28]

---

27   (Arab.) Gos. Inf. 12.
28   Ps.-Mt. 24.

Joseph and Mary got out of there fast and picked up their journey, just in case Afrodisius had a change of mind. Because they left, they were forced to pass through a region that was chock-full of bandits. Another group was traveling through that region at the same time and fell into the hands of those robbers. They were stripped of their clothes, tied up, and robbed of all their possessions. In the meantime, while the heist was underway, Joseph was approaching with his family. Although they were a small group, Jesus was making a lot of noise. It was as if a great man was traveling down the road with a large entourage or an army. The robbers were fearful and figured it would be best to run away. So, that is what they did. They fled, leaving behind the group they had tied up. When Joseph and his family approached, they saw the captives trying to untie each other and gather their belongings. When they saw how small Joseph's group was, they asked: "We figured a large group or an army or something was coming. Where is everyone else? Where is the great man following after you with drums and weapons?" Joseph was surprised and replied: "I do not know; perhaps they are behind us."

They all said goodbye and continued walking, arriving soon at another city. There was a famous demon-possessed girl there. She had gone out one night looking for water and was overtaken by Satan. When the devil entered her, she could not keep her clothes on. She ran all over the place, naked and hurling stones, and insults at people. Her relatives bound her with ropes and chains, but she could not be restrained. She stood at crossroads and among the graves, bringing great terror among the people and grave concerns upon her family. It happened that Mary saw her, realizing instantly what was happening, and felt compassion for her. Mary's desire alone to help this girl caused the demon to flee the body of the girl. She realized she was naked and fled to her home ashamed, yet no one even saw her. Once there, she cleaned up and told her parents about what had happened. They immediately got up and went looking for Mary and Joseph, asking everywhere if anyone had seen the foreigners. When they found them, the parents begged Mary and Joseph to visit their home. They stayed in the house of this family for three days. They just so happened to be the wealthiest family in the city. Afterwards, they continued on their way to the delta, having been well stocked with supplies by the father of the girl who had been demon-possessed.[29]

The road passed through other small towns, where just their presence blessed the people who lived there. We cannot recount them all, but ancient records tell the story of the healing of a young mute that was possessed by several demons, of lepers healed by touching the water that Mary had used to wash the garments of Jesus, etc.[30] Perhaps the most surprising story of all begins with a mule and ends with a lavish wedding. The story goes like this. The family drew near to another city along their journey, and Mary saw three women nearby who were crying. There was a cemetery nearby, so she figured that something terrible had happened and they had just buried a family member. Mary spoke to the girl who was attending to her, saying: "Ask them what happened and see if there is anything we can do to help." The girl did as she was instructed, but the women did not exactly answer the question. Instead, they asked: "Where are you coming from and where are you going?" So, Mary's helper answered: "We are travelers. We have been fleeing from Herod king of Judea. We headed to the delta region, but now we are looking for somewhere to spend the night."

It was customary in their culture to extend an offer of hospitality, so the women offered to open up their home for the weary travelers. They accepted the offer and they all followed with a certain curiosity. When they arrived at their destination, they found a noble and luxurious home, spacious and very nicely furnished, and they made themselves comfortable. Upon entering one of the rooms, Mary's helper saw that there was no one present, only a clean mule covered with a brocade. The three women cared for the mule, providing delicious food and kissing him tenderly.

29   (Arab.) Gos. Inf. 10–14.
30   (Arab.) Gos. Inf. 15ff.

The girl asked what was happening with the mule, and one of the women answered: "We went to bury our father when you came upon us, but we still have this sad circumstance in our own home. This mule is actually our brother. When he came of age, my parents had arranged a wife for him. But there was another woman who wanted him all to herself, and, using trickery, she cast a spell on him. One terrible night while he slept that woman turned him into a mule. And so he remains to this day. We have literally tried everything—we have gone to healers, sorcerers, priests, and magicians. But no one has been able to reverse the spell." The girl replied: "I think the Lord has blessed you this day, because the remedy you have been seeking is now in your home. I used to be a leper. But when the water that the child's mother uses to clean his garments touched my skin, I was instantly healed. Go to Mary and tell her of your grief."

The women were filled with joy at the thought of a cure for their brother. They presented themselves before Mary and recounted the whole story for her. The Virgin then took the child Jesus, led him to the room where the animal was, and put Jesus on him. "My son," she told him, "Have mercy on this family." And as the words left her mouth, the mule changed its shape and gradually transformed into a young man without any blemish. All of them were overjoyed. They were hugging each other and congratulating one another. And then the boy and his sisters fell on their knees, thanking Mary and the child for what they had done for them.

The three sisters said to each other: "This is incredible! He looks exactly as he did when the spell was cast years ago, both in appearance and age. We should go forward then with the wedding plans. How about we give him in marriage to Mary's handmaiden?" The brother and Mary's helper, as if they had been love-struck, nodded with joy at the idea and a lavish wedding was prepared for the couple. They said to Jesus: "Your very presence has turned our sadness and tears into joy."[31]

31   (Arab.) Gos. Inf. 20–22.

Joseph and Mary stayed in that house for ten days. Finally, they left there, though not without some sadness from the relationships they had formed, and came to the city of the delta. For a year they stayed at the home of a widow, paying her a fair amount of money for rent. Jesus reached the age of two while they were living in that home, and he grew in grace and wisdom. One time when he saw some children playing, he went over to play with them. He brought a dead fish from home, threw it into a basin of water, and ordered it to move its tail. The fish came to life and did as it was commanded. Then he put some salt on the fish, and it began to swim like any other fish. A neighbor was looking on and saw what had happened. It was not long before he was telling the widow all about what he had seen. She was fond of the couple and their son, but there was a problem. To host a magician in one's home was punishable in the severest of ways, and she figured it was possible that she had mistakenly done so by allowing this child into her home. Fearful of what the authorities could do to her, she kicked the family out of her home.[32] Finding another home was hard for Joseph. As the days passed, the old man practiced carpentry for the Jews staying in the delta region. And he earned a pretty good living doing so.

All of these things were taking place in Egypt with Jesus. Meanwhile, John and his mother were hiding in the wilderness of Judah. The records do not say exactly how long the two of them[33] stayed in the caves outside of Jerusalem, but they suggest a period of some four or five years, until the death of Herod. Pious Elizabeth died the exact same day as that most hated monarch. John found himself alone at the age of seven. He wept bitterly and did not know how care for and bury his mother's body. At the same time, all the way in Egypt and for no apparent cause, Jesus began to moan as well. His mother asked him: "Jesus, why are you crying? Did your father discipline you?" "No," replied the child. "I

---

32   *Ps.-Thom.* (Lat.) 1:4.
33   *B. Inf. Sav.* 102.

am moaning because Elizabeth has died and left John an orphan. He is crying over her body right now in the mountains."

When Mary heard the news she also began to weep. Jesus encouraged her not to cry. The child summoned a cloud, and it descended upon earth, allowing his mother and a girl, named Salome, to hop on it. The cloud lifted into the air and gently and swiftly carried them to the desert where John was. They embraced him and offered him comfort. Then they prepared Elizabeth's body for burial. Mary wanted to take John with her, but Jesus stopped her: "This is not my Father's will. John will remain in the desert until the appropriate time. And behold, the angel Gabriel will take care of him, providing for him sustenance and protection." Then the cloud returned and carried them back to where they were staying.

Jesus was almost three years old when Herod and Elizabeth died. Records indicate that the king had an incurable disease that caused him severe pain all throughout his body, especially in the stomach region. Not even the baths of Callirrhoe could alleviate his pain. Although he knew his days were numbered, he wanted to end his reign with as much blood on his hands as possible. So, he ordered the execution of his son Antipater, who a few months prior had conspired against him. He ordered the murder of three hundred distinguished people, who were being held prisoner at a racetrack because of their role in the conspiracy. They were executed the same day as Antipater. It is no surprise that Herod's death resulted in great joy throughout Palestine. The news of his death spread like wildfire, even reaching those in Egypt. Joseph learned of Herod's death from an angel, who told him: "Get up, take the child and his mother, and go into the land of Israel, for those who were trying to kill the child are dead."[34] Joseph instantly obeyed. He gathered their belongings, said goodbye to all those who had helped them, and set out. He took Mary with her son and began the journey back to Palestine. Since Archelaus, son of the now deceased and ruthless Herod, was reigning in Judea,

---

34   Matt 2:20.

Joseph was afraid to return to Bethlehem. Instead, he determined to go around as fast as possible and settle in the region of Galilee in a town called Nazareth.[35] The town was not far from Capernaum, and he knew there would be plenty of work for someone with his carpentry skills.

Before they left the country, Jesus issued another warning to those who worshipped idols. In the city of Mesren, Jesus caused another idolatrous temple to collapse.[36] Something very significant happened with this one because the temple was large and surrounded by the city's high walls. The construction of the temple was magnificent, and the first atrium inside had paintings of remarkable quality. This sanctuary was the first temple dedicated to the god Amon and then, with the arrival of the Greeks in Egypt, it had been dedicated to Phoebus Apollo. Jesus and his family passed through the city right when the people were celebrating the annual festival of this god. The people had gathered around the temple compound, which is called a *temenos* (Gr. τέμενος). They brought their gifts and offerings to the idol, which was represented by a beautiful statue of silver and gold. Outside, hecatombs of oxen and white sheep were being prepared, and the masses were going from one place to another in the area around the sacred region. Curiously, Jesus was in the midst of all the hustle and bustle, and he looked very concerned. Suddenly, he read an inscription in Greek, engraved on a wall of the temple, saying: "To Apollo, giver of all good things, who gives life to all mankind." Jesus trembled and anger filled his heart for the great injustice the words communicated by ascribing glory to someone other than his Father. He looked towards heaven and cried aloud: "Father, glorify your son."[37] Some of those present were astonished, wondering how a young child could speak in such a way. Immediately, the whole city began to shake, and the temple

---

35   Matt 2:23.

36   *(Arm.) Gos. Inf.* 15:16–22. The collapse of other temples is mentioned as well; see *(Arm.) Gos. Inf.* 16:1–4; 18:1.

37   John 17:1.

came tumbling down, crushing the priest and servants inside. Some one hundred and eighty people died in the collapse. The people of the city were completely stunned and grieved. Suddenly, there was a great cry throughout the city; a cry of mourning for the dead caught between the stones of the sanctuary erupted throughout the city. Some of those present recalled the strange expression they heard the child speak. The people began to search for him. When they found him, they began to question him about the spell that he had cast, believe it had caused the catastrophe. They asked Joseph: "What are you hiding from us?! We suspect that all of this is because of you and yours!"

They kept pushing with their questions, threatening him in hopes they would get their answers. Mary, who was present, fell down before her son Jesus and begged him not destroy these ignorant people and forgive them instead. At first the child did not want to forgive them. He was angry because they were giving worship to Apollo that should have been directed to his Father. But in the end he succumbed to Mary's intercession and changed his mind. He approached the crowd, as people were mourning for their dead, and he walked among the corpses. Then he raised his voice and so commanded the deceased: "Arise, all of you priests of a vain god!" Immediately, all the servants and priests of Apollo Phoebus stood up and began to walk like sleepwalkers. The mob let out a great shout, hugging him and falling down before him with great admiration, making an attempt to worship him as a supernatural being. But he passed between them and left without uttering a word.

Joseph and Mary were ready to leave the city. In fact, they had already reached the walls of the city. An old man of high repute came running up to them and begged them not to leave the town without first visiting his home. He explained that he had heard that they were Jews. His name was Eleazar, and he was Jewish as well, from Judea, and had fled the Israel because of Herod's violence. That was enough to convince Joseph to accept the invitation and visit the man's home. Once there, Eleazar introduced them to his children—Lazarus, Martha, and Mary.[38] The two families became very close. Joseph and his group stayed in Eleazar's home for three months. Jesus and Lazarus played like two brothers. The eldest two cared for the younger. Martha looked after Lazarus, and Mary after Jesus.

It was during this time that Jesus walked on a beam of light shining forth from the sun. One day, Jesus, Lazarus, and some other children were playing in a room with high ceilings. It was late in the afternoon and the sun was beginning to set. The window was half open, and a ray of light shone through, causing some shadows to form on the floor like a radiant beam. Jesus said to the boys: "Who dares me jump on that beam of light and climb it?" No one said anything. Then Jesus put his arms around the beam of light and started to climb up toward the window.[39] The other kids tried to do the same but to no avail. Upon returning home each of the kids told their parents what they had seen. Joseph heard that the parents found out about what Jesus had done, and he decided to leave because he was afraid it might cause more trouble. So, they set out again on their journey back to Palestine.

---

38   See John 11.
39   (Arm.) Gos. Inf. 15:5.

THE RETURN TO NAZARETH

Joseph decided to return to Palestine, but he wanted to avoid passing through Judea. To do so, he planned the following route: They would cross the desert of Sinai, to the lower end of the Dead Sea, and then move up the other side of the Jordan, to Moab, Ammon, and Gilead, in order to reach Galilee from the West. The whole region was Arab territory, but so far there had been no problems. The route was considered safe.[1] Mary, Joseph, and the child journeyed slowly, walking with their wagon. They were joined by their three servants and Mary's helper. Along the way they stopped when it seemed appropriate, usually in places where other people were and where it was possible to replenish their food and water supplies. When they stopped, Jesus would join the other children and play with them.

On one such occasion, after they entered the land of Moab,[2] Jesus was having fun playing with the other boys on the roof of a house. One of the boys got tired, climbed atop the wall of the terrace, and sat down to rest. It was not long before the boy dozed off. The boy ended up falling off the roof, while the other children were still playing and running around screaming on top of the house. His head hit the floor hard, cracking open his skull and spilling his blood all over the ground. Immediately, his soul left his body. When everyone heard the boy's loud cry, the fun and games immediately ceased. It was a terrifying sight, and all of the

---

1   *(Arm.) Gos. Inf.* 16:1.
2   *(Arm.) Gos. Inf.* 16:1.

children fled in terror. The people of the city picked the boy's dead body off the ground, brought him to his parent's home, and they began to mourn. Later, they met with the children who were playing with their son on the rooftop, and they asked about what had happened. But all the kids said they had no idea.

Obviously, the parents of the dead boy were not happy with this answer, and they made all children appear before a local scribe, who served as a judge. The parents were thinking that the boy had not fallen, but that someone had pushed him and was afraid to say so. The judge interrogated them each one by one. He too was unsuccessful, so he began to threaten them, assuring them that only the culprit would be punished for what had happened. He urged the guilty party to turn himself over. Still when he did not get anywhere, the judge locked the children in a room until they would change their mind and tell the truth. The boys did not know what to do because no one believed their claims of innocence. At that time, one of the older boys had an idea and said to the other boys: "You all know we did not do anything wrong; but they do not believe us. So, let us blame the new boy, Jesus. He is not one of us, but a foreigner. They will condemn him to death, and then we can all go free." They group responded with unanimity: "That is exactly what we should do! Great idea! That is what we will do!"

One of the boys told the judge they were willing to tell the truth. The people assembled very close to where they had placed the corpse of the boy, and all the boys gathered and said: "This foreign child, the son of the old man, is the one who did it. His name is Jesus. He is the one who pushed our friend." Several people set out looking for Joseph. When they found him, they brought him back and pushed him before the judge. He asked Joseph: "Where is your son?" Joseph answered: "What do you want with him?" The judge replied: "Do you not know what this child has done? He pushed a boy off of the roof and the boy died." "As God is my witness," Joseph answered, "I do not know where he is. But I am absolutely sure that he is not responsible for this boy's death."

And at that moment Jesus presented himself before the court. The people were amazed at his demeanor and how he walked. Standing in the middle of everyone, the child asked the crowd: "For whom were you walking around looking?" The people exclaimed: "The son of Joseph, the foreigner!" The judge began to question him immediately: "How could you commit such evil? Tell us." And Jesus calmly began to say to the scribe: "Judge! Do not judge with bias, because it is a sin given your position, not to mention an error against yourself." The scribe was taken aback and replied: "I do not judge you for no reason, but for a reason. The friends of the dead boy, who were with you, have testified against you." So, Jesus responded: "And who testifies to their sincerity?" The judge answered: "They say they are innocent and that you are worthy of death." And Jesus said: "So, if someone testifies against me, we should just trust what they say? What if it turns out that they themselves are afraid to die and have joined together to bear false testimony against me? If so, your verdict would not be fair. They have taken into account that I am not from here. I am a stranger and poor. So, they have shaken the death sentence off of themselves and put it on me. And you, the judge, in order to please the people, assume that they are right and that I am lying."

The judge thought for a moment and then asked: "So, what should I do?" Jesus replied: "Do you want to judge with justice? If so, look for witnesses from both sides and the lie will show itself." The judge said: "I am not as you say. I am only looking for one witness, both for you and for them." Jesus asked: "And if I testify about me, will you believe me?"[3] The judge continued: "Well, how could you prove to me that what you say is true? I will not know if you are swearing with sincerity or lying, and there are many who testify against you." At that moment the other children spoke up and said more or less at the same time: "This boy has done many bad things against us and the children of the city! We have not done anything to him!" The judge said in a firm voice: "See how many witnesses there are against you, and you cannot

---

3   John 5:31.

say anything in return." Jesus was extremely angry. He looked at the judge and spoke in a firm tone: "I have told you many times, and you do not believe me. Now you will see and be amazed." The judge sarcastically replied: "Let us see what you have to say now."

Jesus came to where the dead boy was, took him by the clothes, and said out loud: "Abijah, son of Tamar, get up, open the eyes of these people, and tell everyone how you died." The boy looked as if he was waking up from a dream. He began to move his eyes and recognized some people, calling out to them by name. His parents rushed to him and began to shower him with kisses, asking: "What happened?" And the boy replied: "Nothing." Jesus said to the boy: "Tell us what caused your death. And the child, staring at Jesus, the judge, and his parents, began to speak, saying: "Jesus, you are not responsible for my blood, nor the boys who were with you. I just fell off the terrace. The sun was hot, and I got so tired that I fell asleep. But my friends were afraid of being sentenced to death, so they blamed Jesus."

Jesus with a voice of triumph said to the scribe: "Now do you believe me?" The judge uttered not a word. Likewise, the people were silent in awe of what had just taken place. They were wondering who this child was that possessed such powers. Abijah stood with his parents for three hours, right there, and did not move. After that time, Jesus said: "Abijah, go back to sleep until you wake up in the final resurrection." The boy gently nodded and went back to sleep the sleep of death. Everyone present began to tremble and watched with a mixture of horror and admiration at how the young boy looked dead again. The judge and the boy's parents knelt before Jesus and begged him to bring the boy back to life. But Jesus did not consent to their request. He spoke to the judge, saying: "You unworthy evil magistrate and scribe, how dare you speak of fairness and justice, while you and the whole city, just a moment ago, were ready to condemn me for no reason? Since you have not heard me, I will not hear you." And turning around, without bringing the child back to life, he left everyone dumbfounded.[4]

Joseph told his family they were leaving. During their travels, other wonderful things happened, but it is not necessary to go into as much detail. In a city to the north, in the land of Gilead, Jesus was playing with some children by a river. Jesus turned the water into blood, so that his friends became alarmed. When his playmates became thirsty, he drew some water in a pitcher and gave it to them. He brought it them, and the water had returned to its original state—fresh, crystal clear, and pleasant to the eyes. But when they splashed it on each other, getting it on their clothes, it stained the clothes red as scarlet. And in the next town where Joseph's family stopped, Jesus miraculously cured a boy who had gotten lost in a field and died of thirst and a heat stroke.[5] Elsewhere, Jesus passed the shop of a dyer named Salem, and he went in out of curiosity. Inside there was a lot of cloth waiting to be dyed, arranged in a corner in different piles. Jesus began to play with the fabric, and some got tossed into a container of indigo blue. Salem came and saw the mess—all the fabric had been dyed that one color. The dyer was screaming wildly and grabbed a switch, ready to discipline the child. He said: "What have you done? You have done something terrible, because people wanted these fabrics dyed a certain color, and you have ruined the whole batch." Jesus answered: "I was just playing. Do not worry. I promise I will fix them, all the ones that are the wrong color." He began removing pieces of cloth from the container, and he changed them each to the color that the dyer wanted. As one might expect, the dyer was astonished. He did not say anything, but the gestures he made said it all. He was blown away. And so it was, with many more wonders along the way, until finally the family made their way back to Nazareth.

Life in Nazareth was pretty uneventful, since Joseph returned to the people and the place that he knew. Soon he went back

---

4   (Arm.) Gos. Inf. 16:7–15.
5   (Arm.) Gos. Inf. 17:2–3.

to work and life returned to normal. At the time Jesus was five years old. One day, he was playing with the other children in a stream, which had risen due to recent rains. Jesus built something to redirect the water. He dug seven holes, and they were filled with water. The water was pretty turbulent, but when Jesus looked at it, it calmed and turned clear. Then the child joined together some small dams with rills, and by only his word made the water flow from one to the others. So, Jesus and his companions were entertained when one of the boys, out of envy, closed up the holes out of which the water flowed, so that it overflowed and broke some of the dams of mud, thus ruining what Jesus had built. Jesus was angry and said to him: "Son of death, son of Satan! How dare you undo what I just built?"

And right then the boy fainted and fell over dead. The other children went and told his parents, who hurried to retrieve their son's body, crying the whole way. They left him there and hurried off to where Joseph was, to see if there was something he could do. Joseph, overwhelmed again by what had transpired, said to Mary: "I cannot deal with this. Handle it yourself." His mother came to Jesus and said: "What has this child done to deserve death?" Jesus replied: "He intentionally tore down what I had built." "Jesus," Mary said, "do not be like that. The whole world is upset with us right now." And she tried to convince him with similar points. Jesus calmed down because he did not want to make his mother sad. He went to the home of the dead boy, which was surrounded by a crowd of people. Once there, he touched the buttocks of the corpse and said: "Rise, son of iniquity, you are not worthy to enter the rest of my Father because you tore down what I had built." Then the boy who was dead arose, and Jesus withdrew without giving any explanation.[6]

On another occasion, on the Sabbath, Jesus was playing with his friends near the same stream. He took a little mud from the pond and used it to make twelve sparrows. A neighbor who was passing by was shocked that Jesus would desecrate the Sabbath by

---

6   *Ps.-Mt. 26; Ps.-Thom. 2.*

molding the clay, and he told Joseph: "Your son is in the stream, molding clay, which defiles the sacred day." Joseph came to the place and rebuked Jesus in front of everyone. But the child took little notice, and he did not say a word. Instead, he went to the figurines that he had made and said: "Go. Fly away." At that very moment, the mud was transformed into living flesh, and the clay figurines turned into twelve small, beautiful creatures. The birds began to chirp, took flight, and flew away.

The children took the story home with them. Some parents heard it, and they forbade their children from playing with Jesus in the future, telling them: "Do not play with him. Do not even let him be around wherever you are, for he is just a dangerous magician." The ruler of the synagogue happened to be one of Jesus' fiercest opponents, so much so that on one occasion he locked his own son in the tower of his house in order to prevent him from playing with Joseph's son. He defended his position before the other Pharisees, who were distinguished members of the synagogue, saying: "This Jesus is just doing the same things found in the accounts of the Egyptian Ne-neferka-Path, who picked up some mud, made a boat with rowers, and placed it in the Nile. Then he brought them to life with a spell, and they rowed down the river.[7] This boy is a magician. He probably picked these spells up when he was in Egypt." But Jesus outsmarted the man more than once. One day Jesus was passing by the tower where the boy was being held, and he could hear the boy's voice saying he wanted out. Jesus felt sorry for the boy because his dad had locked him up like a prisoner. There was a small, narrow window on the tower, which allowed just a little light to enter the space. Jesus said to the boy: "Try and slip your hand or even a finger through the window." The child did as he was told, and Jesus grabbed his finger and pulled the boy through the tiny window. They played together and, afterwards, the boy returned to the room through the tiny window.[8]

---

7   Bauer, *Das Leben Jesu*, 96.

8   *B. Inf. Sav.* (de Santos, 221).

When Jesus was about five years old, he was walking down the narrow streets of Nazareth. A boy who was running down the street crashed right into him from behind. Jesus felt a sharp pain from the blow and became irritated. The crash brought the boy to a screeching halt and confused him. Jesus was angry, turned toward the boy, and said: "You shall not continue on your way." The boy immediately fell to the ground dead. The child's parents were furious. They went to Joseph and began to rebuke him harshly, saying: "With a son like this, one of two things must happen. Either you cannot live with us here in this town, or you need to get this child to bless, not curse. Look at what he has done to our son."

The parents were so outraged that they were ready to beat Joseph. For the moment though, they restrained themselves and led him instead to the ruler of the synagogue. Others, who shared the indignation of the parents of the dead boy, stayed close to the house of Jesus, waiting to see what would transpire. Joseph called for the boy, who had returned home, and, trembling, said the following: "Why do you do such things? This just makes people hate us and persecute us." Jesus replied: "These are not your words. Some evil spirit has inspired you to say them. But out of respect to you I will keep quiet. But these others, however, will be punished."

At that moment those who had spoken ill of Jesus went blind. The bystanders were filled with awe and bewilderment. Joseph could not control himself and so he grabbed Jesus by the ear. The boy was angry with Joseph and said: "You already have enough of seeking and not finding. Seriously, by doing this, you are acting crazy. Do not be a cause of affliction to me."[9] Jesus looked around and saw all the indignation against him. In order to prevent a sure altercation, Jesus grabbed the deceased boy by the ear, lifted him up in the air, and began to speak to him. When he did, the spirit of the boy returned to his body and he came back to life.[10] Some

---

9   *Ps.-Thom.* 4:1–5:3.

10   *Ps.-Mt.* 29.

passers-by who saw what happened were aghast and said: "From where did this boy come? Everything he speaks comes to pass."

Soon Jesus was old enough to go to school, and his parents did what was customary among the Jews. In Palestine no child, no matter how small the village where he lived, went without a basic education—reading, writing, and Torah. If by some chance there were no teacher in the town synagogue, the father would be responsible for teaching his children the basics. In Nazareth there was a school in the synagogue, and the teacher there was named Zacchaeus. He had heard many things about Jesus and was interested in having him as a student at the school. Joseph, who knew of Jesus' wisdom, had been somewhat reluctant to send Jesus to school. In fact, other children who were a year younger than Jesus had already begun their studies. One day the teacher found Joseph and said to him: "Why do you not permit your son to study with us? You and Mary are putting your son above the tradition of the elders." Joseph replied: "Do you think someone will be able to direct and educate this boy? He gives the impression like he already knows everything." But Zacchaeus kept insisting, so Jesus ended up going to school.

They were just starting a new round of classes at the school. Zacchaeus struggled to carefully explain to Jesus the rudiments of letters, beginning with Greek and then Hebrew. It was necessary for those living in Palestine to also know the language of the Gentiles because their neighbors in the Decapolis and Syria used it for commerce, as well as religious and cultural events (e.g., theater). He was explaining the sound of all the individual letters, with great care and clarity, and drawing them on a board, from *alpha* to *omega*. Jesus was looking at him intently, and when Zacchaeus paused for questions, Jesus snapped at the teacher: "How dare you try to explain to everyone the *beta,* if you yourself cannot even understand the nature of the *alpha*? You hypocrite, first explain the intimate and true nature of the *alpha*, and then we will believe what you say about the other letters."

Then the child began to question the teacher about the nature of the first letter—why did it have certain traits and not others; what the intersection of the lines meant and shape as a whole; and what the deep meaning of the letter was. He then tried to clarify how truth itself is spiritually hidden in all the letters of the alphabet—the head, he taught, is *alpha*, and *omega* is the neck, the *beta* and *psi* are the shoulder and hands, etc.—and how the whole body, parallel to truth, is represented by the remaining letters.[11] Zacchaeus could not believe what he was hearing. He was baffled by what the boy had said in front of the rest of the class: "Alas! I have no idea what I should do. I am to blame for all this confusion. After all, I am the one who brought the boy to this school." Zacchaeus took the boy back to his father and said: "Joseph, I cannot stand the way he looks at me, nor can I understand anything he says. He has gotten the best of me. I wanted a student and what I got is a teacher, one who I do not follow.[12] But Joseph, you know as well as I do that it would look bad for the child to leave school. I know another teacher, named Levi, in the next village, who is much wiser than me. We should take the boy to him to see if he can teach or mold him into something."

Joseph was not even close to convinced; on the other hand, it made sense that Jesus should not miss school. So, after some hesitation, he consented and agreed to take the child to the next village. The next day, Joseph did so and dropped him off with the other kids at the new school. Jesus went into the school and did not sit with the other children, who were sitting in a circle on the floor. He sat towards the back away from the rest of the students. The teacher, Levi, began his lesson also on the letters, pausing occasionally to ask Jesus questions. But Jesus did not respond. The teacher had been informed about how Jesus was peculiar in many respects, so he decided to exercise a little patience and continued with his lesson plan. At one point in the class, Levi asked Jesus: "Which letter is this, Jesus?" But the boy did not answer. The

11   Irenaeus, *Against Heresies* 1:14:3.

12   *Ps.-Mt.* 30.

teacher was fed up. He grabbed a switch and hit him on his head. When Jesus felt the pain, he angrily turned to the teacher and cursed him. Levi fainted and fell face first on the ground. He did not die, but was he was completely unconscious. They carried him to his house, still unconscious, where he remained so for a number of days. The class was interrupted, and Jesus returned to Joseph's house alone and told him what happened. The old man was filled with regret and decided not to let him leave the house for a while, because everyone who made the child angry basically died or was seriously injured.[13]

A few days passed and Joseph received a visit from an old friend, a teacher in another town. He was a good man and well respected by those who knew him. During their conversation, the teacher pulled out a commentary on the Law and placed it on the table. When Jesus saw the book, he took it and, without even reading the letters on the cover, began to explain the contents of the book to everyone in the house. They were all amazed at the words of wisdom coming from Jesus' mouth and his reasoning. He was so well spoken and his arguments were so logical. The visiting teacher said: "Grace and wisdom flows out of this child." Jesus heard these words, he turned to the teacher and said: "Thank you, for you have spoken with honesty and have given a fair testimony. Because of these words, your fellow teacher will be healed."

And immediately, according to eyewitnesses, the teacher who had fallen into a coma awoke and was completely healed. When Joseph heard that Levi was healed, he was immensely relieved. Joseph knew full well how people who did not really know Jesus could develop a contorted image of him given everything that had transpired. To some Jesus might have looked like an angry, vengeful, insolent, and malicious boy; a know-it-all who was arrogant and uneducated. Apparently, Jesus had become pretty dangerous, and the other children were afraid of him, a sort of rabid and unbearable delinquent. Jesus had become a serious

---

13 *Ps.-Thom.* 14.

concern for both Joseph and his mother, who had to answer for his actions to neighbors and authorities alike.

Although sending Jesus to school did not really work out, life moved on. Jesus used to accompany his father to the carpentry shop, which was always busy. Ancient records reveal at least two interesting stories from inside Joseph's shop. Jesus corrected two of Joseph's mistakes when he miscalculated some measurements. One deals with a very high-end bed that was made of a type of exotic cedar. The cedar itself had to be specially ordered from some Syrian merchants. A rich young man was getting ready to marry a girl from a wealthy family, and he ordered the bed. When the bed was finished and all the materials were used up, Joseph was horrified to see that one of the rails was lower than the rest and one was smaller than the other. Joseph was trying to think of something he could do to fix the problem. It was not an easy fix. It was not like he could just reduce the dimensions of the whole bed. Jesus saw the problem and came to Joseph's aid. He simply nodded his head and immediately the two poles became the same length.[14] Something similar happened with a very special chair, almost like a throne, that was made for a very wealthy person in Jerusalem. This individual specifically went to Joseph to have this piece of furniture made, even though he lived outside the city. He thought highly of Joseph's craftsmanship. The chair took nearly two years to complete. But when it was finished, the measurements were off. Jesus was not worried. He told his father to grab one side and pull, while he did so from the other side. Immediately, the chair was made perfect.[15]

One day Joseph called his son James, who lived with Mary and Jesus, and told him to go to a nearby garden to pick some cabbages for a stew. Jesus went with him. While James was gathering the vegetables, trying to get them the best possible way, a venomous snake slithered through the garden and bit his hand. James was upset and the pain grew so that his hand felt like it

14   *Ps.-Mt.* 41.
15   *(Arab.) Gos. Inf.* 39.

was on fire. He started to feel faint and cried out to Jesus who was nearby watching some birds. Jesus came running. Realizing what had happened, he spoke with a loud voice and the snake showed its face. Jesus commanded it: "Take back all the venom that you put into my brother!" The snake slithered over to James and sucked out all the poison. Afterwards, Jesus cursed the snake and it exploded. Jesus then blew into the hand of James, and it became as it was before the bite.[16]

On another occasion Jesus miraculously restored the foot of a young man who had accidentally severed it with an axe. The man was moments away from death, due to an immense hemorrhage, but the presence of Jesus saved his life. "Arise," the boy said to the man as he lay on the ground dying. "Continue chopping wood, and remember me always." Immediately, the torn limb returned to the man's body, and limb and body were united as they were before. In the same way, he raised some children from the dead and healed others from various diseases, miracles not even worth mentioning here.[17]

Perhaps the most interesting of all these miracles is that of a broken jar. His mother had given it to him to go and fill with water from the spring. Jesus did as he was told, but when he was returning home, he turned the corner and bumped into another child, breaking the pitcher. He went back to the spring sad because his pitcher was broken. When he got there, he decided to use his cloak, filling it with water, and he carried the water that his mother needed back to their home. Seeing what Jesus had done, she began to kiss Jesus, and she treasured in her heart[18] all the mysteries that she witnessed Jesus perform.[19]

Pious Jews who lived outside the capital used to travel to the temple in Jerusalem once a year, during one of the great festivals, usually during the Passover or the Feast of Tabernacles. Joseph was

---

16   *Ps.-Mt.* 41; *(Arab.) Gos. Inf.* 42.

17   *Ps.-Thom.* 17; *(Arab.) Gos. Inf.* 27, 28, 30.

18   Luke 2:51.

19   *Ps.-Mt.* 11.

no exception; indeed, he used to come down every year several times from Galilee. Often several families would travel together to make the trip more manageable. Doing so also made the trip safer from bandits who roamed the roads, especially in Samaria; the Samaritans, by the way, would take every chance they could to rob their Jewish enemies. In one of those return trips, when Jesus was eight years old, a group consisting of his parents and neighbors was traveling the road from Jericho to the north near the Jordan River. Not far from the road, close to the river, there was a deep cave, where a lioness was raising her cubs. The spot was famous because it was not uncommon for hikers to stumble on some of the wild cats in the area. When Jesus was passing by, the lioness had just given birth to four cubs. Right there in front of everyone, Jesus walked straight into the den of the beast. Everyone who saw it wailed. The young lions saw him, ran to him, and began to play, nipping, jumping, and frolicking on the floor. Outside the cave, some distance away, there were a couple of lions. They did not move from where rested; they just wagged their tails at Jesus. Those watching were horrified. Some thought to themselves: "If this boy, or his parents, was so great a sinner, he would not have found himself among the lions." But then Jesus finally came out of the cave and the beasts followed him. The onlookers took off running, hiding wherever they could. Jesus spoke up with a loud voice, so that everyone could hear, saying: "How much better are these animals who recognize who I am and glorify their Lord!" Then he left the beasts and rejoined the group.

Joseph's work increased in Capernaum, so much so that he needed to spend whole seasons there. The family thought it might be better to temporarily move to the city in order to keep the family from being apart so much and, incidentally, eliminate some of the slander occasionally brought about by Jesus' strange behavior.[20] And so they did. Joseph rented a house in Capernaum and the whole family happily moved there. The city was much larger and brighter than the boring town of Nazareth. And

20   *Ps.-Mt.* 40.

Capernaum also had the Sea of Galilee on its doorstep, which was an added attraction, especially for fishing trips. While there, Mary learned of a curious affair where two women were married to the same man. Polygamy, which was not all that uncommon in those days, was prohibited in Palestine, though tolerated by some. Not surprisingly, the Scriptures speak of the ancient patriarchs, such as Jacob and (to some extent) Abraham, as being polygamous, and that God had tolerated their actions. In fact, one could argue that God blessed them in these relationships. Back to the story though. Each of these women had a child, and it happened that both came down with a fever at the very same time. One woman, whose son was named Cleopas, knew of Jesus' power and the influence his mother had on him. She decided to visit Mary and ask for help, offering her a beautiful veil. Jesus' mother gave her in return one of the linens used for the bed of her son. The woman made it into a tunic and put it on the body of her child with the fever. Instantly the fever fled. But the son of the other wife died a few days later. The mother whose child was healed did not even think of giving the linen to the other wife so that her son could be healed as well. Cleopas' mother wanted him to wear it all the time. This caused a lot of resentment between the two women.

The custom in their home was that the wives would alternate household chores each week. It was the mother of Cleopas' turn to do the chores, so she started the necessary work. She lit the oven and went out to get some flour to knead. The other wife, realizing that Cleopas was left alone at home and still angered by what had happened to her own son, threw Cleopas into the oven and ran away. When the mother returned to the home, she noticed that Cleopas was not in the room. She searched and found him smiling amid the flames, playing among them, wearing the tunic that had been made from the material Mary had given her. Immediately, she told the boy to get out of the oven, knowing exactly who had thrown her son into the oven. She took her son and went straight to Mary to tell her all that had happened. Mary told her: "Be careful, and do not say a word, for I fear for you and your child should you tell anyone what I have told you."

The woman followed Mary's good advice. But her opponent was eager to kill her son. On another occasion when the boy was alone near the well, the woman saw that there were no witnesses and threw the boy into the well. She then left and headed to the market. But the plan failed because no harm fell on the child, who was still dressed in the same tunic. He just played with the water in the well and never sank. The mother of Cleopas, meanwhile, was desperately searching for her son, asking all around for his whereabouts and fearing the very worst. Some men who had visited the well for water found the boy floating down inside. They lifted him out of the well and gave him to his mother. Again the mother of Cleopas ran to Mary and told her all about what had transpired. She was more afraid than ever that sooner or later this woman was going to succeed in killing her child. Mary replied: "Do not fear, because God will take care of this matter and he will take vengeance for you."

It was not long before the other woman had to go to the well to draw some water. Somehow, her feet got caught on the rope and she tripped on the rim of the well, which was very low to the ground. She fell into the well. Her husband and the other men of the city were not far off, and they could hear her screams. They ran to pull her out. They succeeded in getting her out, but they found that she had suffered a terrible head injury as well as some broken bones. There was nothing they could do for her, and she died two days later.

Not only did Jesus' clothes have such powerful effects on people, but also the water that had touched his body or clothing. There are stories of lepers being cured and people with other types of diseases, some we already know about from the trip to Egypt. And these were repeated in Israel, including the casting out of demons. But there is little space to repeat those accounts here.[21]

---

21   (Arab.) Gos. Inf. 22:31–34.

The last of the great wonders of Jesus' childhood took place when he was twelve, as recorded in the Gospel of Luke.[22] Jesus rubbed shoulders with teachers and scholars of Israel, asking questions regarding their own specialties, including astronomy and physics, and fielding questions directed towards him. But after his return to Nazareth-Capernaum, Jesus began to hide his miracles and live under the radar of both men and devils, busy with his work as a carpenter and the study of the Law.[23] This is why not much can be said of his life from the period of time when Jesus was twelve until he was thirty years of age. He had decided to conceal his life from the eyes of all who were alive.

---

22 Luke 2:40–52.

23 *(Arab.) Gos. Inf.* 40–44.

THE DEATH OF JOSEPH

Joseph approached the end of his life when Jesus was eighteen years old. Jesus shared about Joseph's last moments with his disciples on the Mount of Olives. He also shared with them a little about his hidden life, especially concerning the old man who had cared for him and his mother. One of his disciples wrote down some of what Jesus shared with them on the Mount of Olives that day,[1] writing it down on a beautiful manuscript that was later placed in the library in Jerusalem. On it was written the date of Joseph's death—the twenty-sixth day of the Egyptian month Epap, which is the twentieth of July, in the forty-second year of Augustus' reign.

Although Joseph was a very old man, about 111 years old, his body was not weak, his vision was not poor, and there was not a single jagged tooth in his mouth. Mentally he was all there, and his decisions were always guided by the clearest reasoning. But he finally succumbed to the fate of all mankind and his body fell sick. Just as an angel had warned Abraham, so an angel did with Joseph, telling him that he would die that year. But, of course, Joseph—it is said—was not as disobedient as Abraham who, upon receiving the news of his early death, made it clear that he was not willing to follow the angel of the Lord, Michael, into the next world.[2]

---

1   The *History of Joseph the Carpenter* serves as the basis for this whole chapter.
2   *T. Ab.* 7:11.

Joseph, before his passing, simply made a trip to Jerusalem to say goodbye to the temple of the Lord.

Near death, in the presence of God, Abraham confessed of all of his sins and repented of everything that he thought he had done wrong. His conscience was sensitive, so sensitive he even confessed trespasses that he had not actually committed. Then he prayed to God that the archangel Michael would not depart from him in the bitter sleep that was approaching. Thus, his soul could leave the body without pain or embarrassment and pass from this life to being in the presence of God. In those days, people believed that demons were stationed along the pathway from this life to the next. Joseph believed this as well. The demons attempted to scare the souls on their journey, and fear was felt as these souls passed by the keeper of hell or the waves of the river of fire. The souls had to get through unscathed before reaching God.[3] So, he prayed: "O God! Do not permit my soul to fall into the hands of the keeper of hell and do not fill me with confusion in your court. Do not let the waves of the river of fire, which is hell itself, become angry with me. O God, who judges everyone in truth and justice, I hope that your love will be my comfort, because you are the source of all that is good, and to you belongs all the glory, forever and ever! Amen."

The disease progressed quickly. It was not long before it affected his mind, and he forgot to eat and drink, and the skill he had as a carpenter began to fade. At dawn on the twenty-sixth of Epep, Joseph's condition worsened as he lay on his bed. He began to cry out: "O wretched me! Cursed is the day that my mother brought me into this world!"

As Joseph drew nearer to the end of his days, some things in his past began to haunt him, brought about by his more sensitive conscience, and he began to dread the moment when he would stand before the divine court. He began to shout: "Woe to my tongue and my lips, for they have uttered insults, deceit, slander,

---

3   *Hist. Jos. Carp.* 13.

and calumny! Woe to my eyes, for they have seen disgrace! Woe to my ears, for they have willingly listened to frivolous speech!"

His outburst could have extended to other parts of his body—his hands, his feet, his stomach—and all their imperfections from the distant past, but he did not. Instead, his soul calmed, and he said: "You, Jesus, God, you are my lawyer. And may your divine will be accomplished in me."

Jesus appeared at his father's bedside, reminding him that every human being must at some point go to the Father and that, in his case, there was nothing to fear. Once out of his father's sight, Jesus was moved to tears, watching how his father was close to death. It reminded him too that he would suffer a cruel death on the cross at the hands of the Jews, although his own death would result in life for the world.

Meanwhile, Mary could not understand why Joseph needed to suffer the fate of all mankind. "Is the good and blessed old man, Joseph, going to die?" she asked. Jesus answered: "Nobody who lives, not even yourself, will escape this fate. But take heart. We do not need to call it death, rather it is the passage to eternal life. I too must suffer this fate because I have taken on mortal flesh."

Throughout this whole time Jesus stood at the head of Joseph's bed and Mary at his feet. Joseph fixed his eyes on the face of Jesus, sometimes unable to utter a word, other times only able to groan. Jesus massaged his hands and feet. He placed his hand once on the old man's chest to quiet his soul. And Joseph rested.

Some the sons and daughters from a previous marriage came to visit Joseph during the end. One named Lisia dared to speak out and told her brothers: "I swear, dear brothers, that this is the exact same disease that afflicted our mother, and now here it is again. Our father has it, and we are not going to see him again until we see him in eternity." Then everyone burst into tears again, and they went to be with Jesus and Mary.

It was not long before Death showed up with a group of demons, looking at Joseph like an angry, rabid animal. Only Joseph could see them, and he just knew that they had come hoping to take his soul. Jesus prayed to his heavenly Father at that moment and asked: "Father, send me a host of angels, including Michael, the administrator of your goods, and Gabriel, the great messenger of light, to accompany the soul of my father Joseph. And I pray that they will not have to travel those hellish, terrible roads because they are infested with evil spirits."

Immediately, a whole host of good angels appeared. Joseph's face was relieved when he saw that the good angels outnumbered the evil ones. The latter were waiting for the moment of his death with great anticipation. Jesus said to Joseph: "Father, you will not to travel the hellish pathways, nor will you have go through the dreadful place where the river of fire churns like the waves of the sea. No, the angels of my Father are going to keep you safe in his mighty hand."

When Joseph breathed his last breath nobody even noticed, except Jesus who was sitting by his bedside. The angels took his soul and wrapped it in silk linens. The Savior recommended that Michael and Gabriel serve as guards of Joseph's soul, in order to protect him from the evil spirits lying in wait against him. And so it happened. The soul of Joseph was transferred directly to the presence of God without having to take a single difficult path, through which all other mortals had to pass. The angels, meanwhile, began to sing songs of praise as the soul of the patriarch appeared before the Eternal Father. Then Jesus said to everyone present: "Joseph is no longer in this world. He has died. But his death is not death, but life everlasting." And everyone was amazed because they had not even noticed the moment that he passed. Jesus' siblings tore their clothes and wept for a long time.

Jesus then blessed the body of his father and ordered two angels to wrap his body in a shroud. The whole town of Nazareth grieved. There were mourners wailing for the loss of Joseph from dawn until the ninth hour, that is, until late afternoon. Jesus cried aloud to those present: "I will not allow his body undergo decay, nor suffer corruption. It will remain intact until the day of the first resurrection, when the martyrs rise and reign with me for a thousand years of heavenly kingdom of God on earth.[4] And as for all those who honor the memory of my father on earth, either with alms or by giving their children his name, I will make it so that when they leave this world, their sins shall be blotted out of the heavenly book, and they shall not undergo any torment."

A little while later, the elders of the city, along with the undertakers, arrived at Joseph's home to conduct the funeral. There they found the body of the patriarch Joseph. His shroud was so well made to the contours of his figure. It looked as if it had been fastened with iron clamps. And when they removed his body, they did not find a single opening in the shroud. It was perfectly made. And so they took his body to the family tomb, where he was buried next to his father Jacob.

When they were placing the body in the grave, Jesus touched it, remembering everything that the good old man had done for him, from the flight into Egypt all the way to the present, especially how he had cared about his mission for so many years. He ordered the gravediggers to stop and, leaning over the body of the old man, he wept for a long time. Then he cried out: "O Death, the tears and the pain you are causing! But this power you have comes from the One who rules over the whole universe. But my resentment is not so much against Death as it is against Adam and Eve, who by failing to submit to the divine will fell into sin. If Adam had not been disobedient, my Father in heaven would not have punished him with this terrible scourge. And I, having also took on this flesh, I too must die so that I can have mercy on the creatures that I formed."

When Jesus' apostles heard this story from his Jesus' own lips, they said to their Master: "We thank you, Lord and Savior, for sharing all of this with us. But we do not fully understand it. How can the one who granted immortality to Elijah and Enoch, who did not have to die, do this very thing to Joseph? Jesus answered: "I tell you, there will come a time that they too must also die. The sentence pronounced by my Father to Adam will not pass by even

---

4   Rev 20:4–6.

them. They will die in a day of confusion, fear, and cries of doom and grief. You should know that the Antichrist will kill these two men and pour out their blood on the ground like water from a glass."

And with that the disciples understood that Jesus was referring to the time before the end of the world. They remained calm and praised Jesus and his Father.

THE PUBLIC MINISTRY OF JESUS

After the death of his adoptive father, Jesus basically went twelve years without leaving Nazareth. He inherited his father's customers, and business was good. The rest of his time was devoted to the study of the Law and meditating on it. When a protector of the Torah appeared in Galilee, aggravating the people with his preaching, Jesus gladly went to listen. But overall, those days were pretty uneventful. The only interesting thing was that Simeon and James were married, so that Mary and Jesus were alone at home. Jesus took care of all the wedding plans, as if they were his own children.

When Jesus turned thirty, he knew that the time had come for him to leave his hiddenness and communicate to all Israel that which had been maturing inside him all these years. At first, he would just go and listen to the sermons of John the Baptist, his cousin, until one day he too became one of John's disciples. And so began his public life. But the existence of the "other Jesus" at this important stage of life keeps us steeped in the greatest of mysteries. The reason is simple—the old records used here to study the life of Jesus barely treat this period of time, primarily because it was covered relatively well in the canonical documents. Therefore, the other documents, not found in the New Testament, tip toe over the parts of his life covered elsewhere to report something new to its readers.

These documents are not particularly interested in the appearance, body, or shape of Jesus at this time of his life. Actually, the data is not consistent from one source to another. For some, Jesus was extremely ugly, so that the prophecy of Isaiah was fulfilled: "He has no stately form or majesty that we should look upon him, nor appearance that we should be attracted to him."[1] For others, Jesus was a beautiful and handsome man, more so than anyone before or after.[2]

The first event we have any news about is the baptism of the Nazarene by John. As we know, John the Baptist had made the desert his home and his diet consisted of locusts and wild honey.[3] What is most interesting, though, is God gave the honey a special taste; it was equal to the manna that the Israelites had eaten as they journeyed through the desert for forty years, like a cake dipped in oil.[4] John was confident as an adult from his meditations and his relationship with God that the end of the world was near, and he went about preaching the immediate coming of God's judgment on all the nations, the kingdom of God, and the need to prepare for it.[5] One of the preparations, other than penance and a willingness to comply with the Law, was the act of being baptized as a sign of repentance for past sins and turning a new leaf for the future.[6] And so John was baptizing in the Jordan those people who were convinced by his preaching of the imminent and terrible judgment that was coming upon the world.

Many people came to him from Jerusalem, including some from the sect of the Pharisees, who considered themselves just about perfect. Even Jesus, when he was thirty years of age, on November 8th,[7] or possibly January 6th,[8] made the decision

---

1   Isa 53:2; see Justin, *Dialogue with Trypho* 14, 49, 85; Irenaeus, *Against Heresies* 3:19:2; 4:33:12; Tertullian, *On the Flesh of Christ* 9; etc.
2   See Clement of Alexandria, *Stromata* 2:5:21; *Acts John* 73, 74.
3   Mark 1:6.
4   *Gos. Eb.* 4 (de Santos, 51).
5   Luke 3:7.
6   Matt 3:7ff.
7   Cf. the testimonies of Epiphanius, *Panarion* 51:16, 24, 28.
8   Cf. Clement of Alexandria, *Stromata* 1:21:146.

to be baptized by the passionate preacher after his mother and his brothers encouraged him to do so. At first he was not very convinced of the need for such a baptism. They told Jesus: "John is baptizing people for the remission of their sins. Let us also go out to where he is and be baptized by him." Jesus did not like the whole idea and replied: "What sins have I committed, for which I have need to be baptized? That is, unless what I have said is wrong and I am mistaken."[9]

It could be said that the material body of Jesus (also called the "psychic" body by the Gnostics)[10] might have actually needed some purification.[11] Be that as it may, the fact is, according to our documents, Jesus was persuaded by his mother to go down to the Jordan.[12] Strangely, John did not recognize Jesus when he arrived, even though John was his cousin.[13] Nevertheless, the events about to transpire would let him know full well who it was that had come to be baptized. The patriarch Levi had already prophesied that Jesus would be baptized in a writing known as the *Testament of Levi*. The following words were uttered on his deathbed: "The heavens will open and, from the glorious temple, sanctification will fall on him with the Father's voice, just as the voice of Abraham spoke to Isaac. To him will be given the glory of the Most High, and the Spirit of wisdom will rest on him in the water."[14]

When it came time for Jesus to be baptized, John motioned for him to come out to the middle of the river. It was already

---

9   *Gos. Naz.* 31 (de Santos, 42, which attributes it to the *Gospel of the Hebrews*). On the different attribution of the fragments, see Piñero, "Los Evangelios apócrifos."

10   There are three parts to man, according to the Gnostics: the corporeal (or "hylic"), the part endowed with a soul ("psychic"), and the spiritual (or "pneumatic"). Only the latter is capable of binding with divinity, since it is consubstantial with divinity and is not affected by the material in any way.

11   *Pistis Sophia* 59.

12   *Preaching of Paul* (collected by Pseudo Cipriano, *De rebaptisme* 17 [de Santos, 43ff.]).

13   John 1:31.

14   *T. Levi* 18:6–7. See Piñero, *Apócrifos del Antiguo Testamento V*, 60.

springtime and hot, so it was not inconvenient at all to get one's clothes wet in the sacred waters. John put his hand on the head of Jesus and pushed him down with some force, so that the waters would cover him all at once for a moment. As he stood up, the heavens tore open, and everyone saw a white dove descend from the sky and enter him. This signified that all the power of the Spirit rested on him and had been placed inside him. "My Son," he said, "all this time, out of all of the prophets, I have been waiting for you, so that I could dwell inside you. For you are my rest, my firstborn Son, who reigns forever."[15] And so everyone present could understand, a powerful voice from heaven spoke, rumbling like thunder: "Today I have begotten you. You are my beloved Son. In you I am well pleased."

John could not believe what he saw and heard. He asked Jesus: "Who in the world are you?" But Jesus did not answer; instead the voice from heaven answered for all to hear, saying: "This is my beloved Son." Immediately, a great white light lit up the whole place,[16] and a great fire began to burn on the water.[17] John simply did not know what to do; nothing like this had ever happened with any of the hundreds of people, thousands even, that he had baptized. He immediately threw himself down at the feet of Jesus and said: "Baptize me, Lord, I beg you." But Jesus refused. In a very soft voice, he said: "It is proper to fulfill all righteousness."

And for a moment the whole body of the Nazarene became visible, radiant and beautiful, as if it was wearing a garment of light.[18] After a while, Jesus withdrew from that place, but the white clouds remained for a long period of time. Some were privileged to see a choir of angels in the sky, who sang hymns of praise to God. They also noticed how the Jordan momentarily stopped flowing

15   *Gos. Eb.* 28 (de Santos, 41).
16   Variant of Codex Vercellensis (fourth century) and Codex Sangermanensis (seventh century) for Matt 3:13–17 (de Santos, 108, 110).
17   *Preaching of Paul* (collected by Pseudo Cipriano, *De rebaptisme* 17 [de Santos, 43ff.]).
18   *Pistis Sophia* 63.

and remained calm; and when the waters continued their normal course, a wonderful smell, the best tuberose scent, spread along the banks of the river.[19]

And that is how Jesus began his public life. The next event in his life was the temptation. All divine messengers must be tested before starting their work, and Jesus was no exception. The records show that the devil was not the originator of the temptation. The Holy Spirit was commissioned to put Jesus within reach of the Tempter, showing that the temptation was by divine permission, not an imposition of Satan. Indeed, the Spirit—according to some documents, the true mother of Jesus[20]—took Jesus by the hair, as he had done before with Habakkuk[21] or Ezekiel,[22] and took him to the top of Mount Tabor, where he was tempted and subsequently triumphed over the devil.[23]

The next step was choosing the disciples.[24] Jesus acted sovereignly: It was decided in advance who would be deemed the best and most suitable for such an important mission, those whom his Father had chosen for him.[25] They were the same disciples who later shared about the event.[26] Jesus was about thirty years old,[27] and he arrived in Capernaum. He had already preached many times in the area and his fame spread by word of mouth. Some were really taken in by what he was preaching, and they were willing to follow Jesus as disciples. Jesus entered Simon's house and said to him: "While I was walking on the shore of Lake Tiberias, I chose John and James, the sons of Zebedee, to be my

---

19   Variant of Tacitus' *Diatessaron* (Bauer, *Das Leben Jesu*, 140).

20   *(Cop.) Gos. Heb.* 5 (de Santos, 35).

21   In *Bel* 36 (expansion of the Septuagint version of Daniel), it is an angelic spirit that makes the transfer.

22   Ezek 8:3.

23   Matt 4:1–11.

24   Mark 3:13–19.

25   *(Cop.) Gos. Heb.* 13 (de Santos, 39).

26   *Gos. Eb.* 2 (de Santos, 50).

27   Luke 3:23.

disciples. I also want you to be one of my disciples, Simon. I want to have twelve disciples, the same number as the number of the tribes of Israel, to serve as a testimony unto them."[28] And so it happened, Simon, leaving his home and his family, decided to follow the Master.

Some time had passed since the beginning of his public ministry and Jesus went to the synagogue in Capernaum. During the worship service on the Sabbath, after praying together, they would read various sections of the Law and the Prophets in Hebrew. The common language in Palestine was Aramaic, which had been imposed throughout the Middle East since the region had become part of the Persian Empire. Because of that, the people who assembled in the synagogue did not understand the sacred language. Therefore, they were in the habit of translating and paraphrasing the Hebrew in Aramaic. After the reading from Scripture, a short message was offered, the sort of message that could have been given by anyone in those days, provided they had the necessary knowledge and interest to do so. Jesus took the opportunity that Saturday to teach in the synagogue and expand everyone's understanding about the kingdom of God. He even did some miracles of healing there.

One Sabbath there was a man who had a withered hand. Everyone was watching Jesus to see if he would heal on the Sabbath. The man had heard that the Nazarene did many miracles and healings, so it seemed like a good opportunity to ask Jesus to heal him. He addressed Jesus with these words: "Dear sir, please hear my request. I know that you can heal people. I have a family and am a bricklayer, and so I earned a living by working with my hands. For me my hands are all that I have. I beg you, please restore my hands so that I do not have to beg for a living."[29] Jesus was persuaded by the man's points, and he healed him right there, not phased a bit by what people might say about it being a so-called violation of the Sabbath.

---

28   *Gos. Pet.* 14 (60); *Did. Apost.* 31; *Gos. Mary* (de Santos, 97).
29   *Gos. Naz.* 23 (de Santos, 40).

Now this does not mean that Jesus did not respect the sacredness of the Sabbath or that he would just violate it on a whim. On another occasion, far from the city, Jesus saw a man who was plowing his field on the Sabbath. Jesus walked up to him and said: "Man, if you only knew what you are doing and knew the deep meaning of the Sabbath, blessed you would be; but if not, you are cursed and a transgressor of the Law."[30]

Jesus also had a very heated discussion with the Pharisees, who afterwards decided to do away with their annoying adversary in the most expeditious and secure way possible.[31] They stirred up a mob against Jesus, and, when they were all set to go, the leaders came to place him under arrest him and hand him over to the mob with his hands bound. Though there were many, still they could not arrest him. He slipped away as they were trying to take hold of him, and no one could figure out how. This happened several times, until the mob finally gave up. And Jesus withdrew from them.[32]

Jesus left with his disciples. As he was going away, a leper came up to him and said: "Master Jesus, I contracted leprosy because I went with a group of lepers and ate together with them in the inn. But if it is your will, I can be healed of this infirmity." The word "leprosy," by the way, did not mean the same as it does today (e.g., a garment of clothing[33] or a wall[34]), but to any kind of skin disease, which meant there could be many "lepers" in Palestine. Jesus, full of compassion, looked at him and replied: "I will it so. Be clean. Now go and show yourself to the priests." And immediately he was healed of the disease.[35]

On another occasion when Jesus was walking along the banks of the Jordan River, there was a heated discussion between

---

30   Variant of Codex Beza Cantabrigensis (fourth century) in Luke 6:4.
31   John 5:18.
32   Egerton Papyri 1 (front side), 23ss.
33   Lev 13:47–59.
34   Lev 14:34–48.
35   Egerton Papyri 1 (front side), 30–42.

him and some people from Jerusalem about the possibility of a resurrection. This was a hot-button theological issue at the time since the Law and the Prophets supposedly "never deal with the topic." Quite the contrary. The ancient Scriptures implied quite clearly that human life ends in this world. In other words, there is no otherworldly life. Life ends when it comes to its natural end. Over time, however, before the time of Jesus and the influence of philosophical and religious ideas from outside Palestine (especially from the Greek world), the notion of the immortality of the soul and the resurrection of the body had been making headway among the Jews, especially among the "pious" and the Pharisees. But the more traditionalists who clung to the pure text of the Old Law did not believe in such advances, nor did they believe that Yahweh had guaranteed or promised such wonders. The opponents of Jesus, called the Sadducees, did not agree with any of his arguments. This group wholeheartedly denied the possibility of a bodily resurrection, saying there would be nothing left of the physical body by the time of such a resurrection at the end of the time. Then Jesus, with the intention of showing that nothing was impossible with God, stood on the riverbank and asked one of his companions for a few grains of wheat that he had in his saddlebag. Jesus planted them in the middle of the stream. After a short time, in front of everyone present, robust stalks with thick heads of grain rose out of the water. The men went over to the stalks, picked them, and threshed the wheat that was in them, which was of excellent quality.[36]

It was near the last time that Jesus would go up to Jerusalem. He took his three favorite disciples—Peter, James and John[37]— and went to the mountain where he used to pray.[38] He pulled back from them and began to pray alone. John, who was a rather curious man, inched closer to where Jesus was without him noticing. And then John saw something marvelous. A bright light

---

36   Egerton Papyri 2 (back side), 63–73.
37   Mark 9:1–13.
38   *Acts John* 90ff.

shone around the Master and a powerful voice spoke something that he did not quite understand.[39] Then, in recounting the episode to his companions, who had seen nothing, he could not even find the words to describe how marvelous was the scene. And then, on another day, Jesus did the exact same thing with the three disciples. When they reached the mount, Jesus left them to pray. This time, the radiance that shone around Jesus was perfectly visible from a distance. Again, John was the only one to draw near, since the other two disciples were afraid to budge. What he saw was indescribable: Jesus looked naked, not as a human being but as something different, much bigger. His feet were like glowing snow, while the ground beneath his feet shone brightly, and his body was so enormous that his head reached up to heaven.

The disciple was uncontrollably afraid and began to scream out. For a moment, he thought that Jesus was going to wipe him off the face of the earth. By the time he had accepted his fate, the Master turned to him and something wonderful happened—his figure changed back to normal. He was no longer great and tall with his head reaching into the heavens. He took John by the chin and lifted him from the ground, saying: "Do not be unbelieving, but believing; and do not be indiscreet." John apologized and replied: "But what have I done, Lord?" The truth is Jesus had hurt him when he took him by the chin. It hurt for thirty days. Daringly, John said to the Master: "If a soft tap from you, without even being serious, has caused me so much pain, what would it have been like had you really hit me?" Jesus answered him, saying: "In the future, try not to tempt he who cannot be tempted."

Peter and James watched from afar as John talked with Jesus. They were motioning to him that he should leave the Master alone. John heeded their warnings, having just been rebuked by the Master, and he went back to where Peter and James were. His two companions asked: "Who were those two men who were talking to Jesus on the mount?" John asked: "What are you talking about?" That was strange. John had not seen Jesus talking to two

---

39   *Acts Pet.* 20.

individuals, so he could not answer their question. He understood, however, that Jesus was a mysterious being, who no one could fully comprehend and who was displayed in many different ways according to how each one could understand him.[40] So, John answered the two other disciples: "I have not seen anyone. But if you ask him, he will surely tell you what you want to know."[41] One thing, however, that I can tell you is sometimes you could touch it—like his body was physically there—and sometimes you could not—it was there, but you could not have touched it if you tried. Sometimes I walked behind him to see his footprints on the ground, but I noticed that he walked just a little above the ground so that he left no tracks."

On another day, in Capernaum near the Sea of Galilee, Jesus and his disciples were all sleeping on the floor in a large room of a home that a follower of the Master had made available to them. They were worn out from all the day's events, and all fell into a deep sleep, except for John. The disciple was wrapped up well in a blanket, but he was awake and watching Jesus' every move. Jesus said to him: "John, go to sleep." John pretended to sleep, but he kept watching. Then suddenly, a mysterious figure appeared next to Jesus that closely resembled the Master. Although the two of them were talking low, John could still hear some of what they said. At one point the mysterious companion said to the Master: "Jesus, those whom you have chosen as followers do not believe in you." Jesus did not really pay it any mind, saying: "True, but they are just men.[42]

That is how the days passed during Jesus' public ministry. The canonical writings have preserved a record of many of the events of Jesus' life. Jesus led a stern, humble, and poor life,[43] giving all his time to preaching the coming kingdom. He had no objection to spending his time with sinners or to accept an invitation to

40 *Acts Pet.* 20.
41 *Acts John* 90–91.
42 *Acts John* 92.
43 *Acts John* 113; *Pistis Sophia* 100.

dine in the home of one of the distinguished Pharisees. He was completely impartial. But Jesus never ate meat when he dined with people. He was a committed vegetarian.[44] Once it so happened that he was invited to dine with a Pharisee. The lady of the home started to offer bread to each guest. She offered bread to Jesus, and he took a piece. After taking it, he blessed it and, without giving time for the others to take a piece of bread, he had divided his bread among those present. There were more than twenty people, and they were all filled just from the portions they received. No one needed to bring any more food to the table.[45] Jesus' total abstinence from meat also clarifies something he said about his mission in the world: "I have come to abolish sacrifices, and, if you do not stop sacrificing, I will not turn my anger away from you."[46] The allusion to the victims is explained because the priests, and part of the people, eat the meat after the animal is sacrificed, reserving for God alone all of the skin, fat, and bones. These are consumed on the altar; the rest was used as food.

Jesus' fame spread to every corner of Palestine and beyond as a result of his healing miracles. The records tell the story of Abgar V, king of a small remote region called Osroene, which is located beyond the Euphrates, and how news of Jesus reached even him. Abgar contracted leprosy and was desperate because it forced him to withdraw and prevented him from being seen in public. None of the delights of his palace in Edessa could satisfy him. One day, one of the palace suppliers delivered goods from the West (from Tyre and Sidon) via camel. Sometimes that merchant would make trips down to the Decapolis. Anyways, he told the king about a new prophet in Galilee and how he was healing people left and right. The king wanted to see Jesus. He wanted to beg Jesus to heal him. He declined to make the trip, though, because it seemed inappropriate to put off all of his work in the kingdom. Instead, he decided to send Jesus a letter and request that Jesus visit him.

---

44   *Gos. Eb.* 7 (de Santos, 52).

45   *Acts John* 93.

46   *Gos. Eb.* 7 (de Santos, 52).

Through his personal courier, named Hannan, the king sent Jesus the following message:

> *Abgar, king of Edessa, to Jesus, the great prophet who has appeared in Galilee:*
>
> *News about you has reached me. People are saying that you heal the sick without the use of drugs or herbs. They are saying the blind see, the lame walk, lepers are made clean, and demons are being cast out of those who are possessed. You heal those who have been tormented by all sorts of diseases and even bring the dead back to life.*
>
> *When I heard this report, I thought it was one of two things. Either you yourself are a god, who has come down from heaven to perform these wonders here on earth, or you are the child of a god who has the power to do such wonders. Here now is the reason why I am writing to you. I beg you, please come to me and heal me of this affliction that I have.*
>
> *I have also heard that your fellow Jews murmur against you and seek to do you wrong. My city is very small, but noble, and there is plenty of room for you here.*[47]

The messenger had no difficulty delivering the letter to Jesus in Galilee. He presented the letter to him along with a very beautiful present from the king, a scroll of the Torah, the first five books of the Jewish Scriptures, which the monarch had purchased from a Jewish scribe in Babylon. The scroll was of the highest quality and the calligraphy the best of the best, fit for a king. But Jesus, who had accepted the messenger with some hesitancy because he was an impure pagan, rejected the gift. He read the letter carefully and was impressed by the king's faith. Many Jews had listened to him preach about the kingdom and seen him do many wonders, but still their hearts remained closed. The next day Jesus asked Hannan for some writing materials and he penned the following reply to the king:

---

47   Eusebius, *Ecclesiastical History* 1:13:15 (de Santos, 662).

*King Abgar, blessed are you because you believed in me
without having ever seen me.[48] Those who have seen me do
not believe in me. And others, who have not seen me, will
believe in me and have life.*

*Regarding your request for me to come to you, I cannot.
I must stay here and fulfill the purpose for which I have been
sent. When all of it is fulfilled, I will return to the one who
sent me.[49] But when I get there, I will send you one of my
disciples to heal you of this illness and give life to you and
yours.[50]*

The messenger was disappointed. He figured Jesus would have
granted the king's request. Taking the letter, he asked Jesus if he
would let him paint a portrait of him. Hannan was a gifted painter
and had brought with him all the necessary painting instruments.
Jesus did not expressly grant him permission, but he did not exactly
refuse either. The next day Hannan joined Jesus and his disciples
at the home of Gamaliel the Pharisee for dinner. Looking in from
a neighboring room, Hannan painted that portrait of Jesus. It was
not perfect, since it had been made in haste and Jesus had not
stood still for a moment. But it was good enough to show the king
the poise and grace of the Nazarene. With regard to Jesus' promise,
indeed, shortly after the death of Jesus, Thomas urged Thaddeus
to go to that region and preach the gospel there. He healed the
king of his leprosy, and he baptized many people in that region,
changing its name to Addai. Later, an anonymous chronicler wrote
the so-called *Doctrine of Addai*, which contains this story and the
story of the conversion of Osroene to Christianity.

The records say little more about the public life of Jesus. There
is the interesting story that the donkey, which Jesus rode during his
triumphant messianic entry into Jerusalem, was descended from

---

48   John 20:29.
49   John 13:20; 14:3–4.
50   John 13:20; 14:3–4.

Balaam's donkey,[51] bringing to a close a long lineage of donkeys that served the prophets. Following all these glorious moments, Jesus entered the most important week of his life. The clash with the leaders of the people, and the Romans, had reached its apex when Jesus entered the holy city as the Messiah.[52] The subsequent conflict with the authorities, which would set everything into motion, was anything but unexpected. Passover was approaching and since Jesus and his disciples were from Galilee, they had to find somewhere in Jerusalem to celebrate the holy day. His disciples asked him: "Teacher, where do you want us to prepare for you to eat the Passover?" Jesus answered them: "Do I wish to eat meat with you this Passover?"[53]

Jesus' answer meant a significant change to the entire Jewish tradition. According to the previous discussion of Jesus' vegetarianism, Jesus was going to celebrate the Passover without sacrificing a lamb, which was mandatory. And so it was. The disciples found a suitable place and made the appropriate preparations,[54] but this Passover meal consisted of nothing more than bread and water. There was also no glass of wine, even though it was a mandatory component to the celebration. Jesus, who acted as the father of the group, blessed the food and prayed the customary prayers. After the first part of the ceremony, bread and water were distributed to everyone present. The bread was dipped in bitter herbs and the atmosphere was rather sad, full of tension and fear. Martha and Mary, friends of Jesus who lived in Bethany and whose brother Lazarus had been raised from the dead, wanted to observe the Passover with them. Although it was only meant for the closest disciples, namely the twelve, these two women were granted permission. James, the brother of the Lord, was there too as a special guest, even though he was not one of Jesus'

---

51   *Acts Thom.* 40.

52   Mark 12:12–19.

53   *Gos. Eb.* 7 (de Santos, 52); *Gos. Marcion* (Passover), cf. Bauer, *Das Leben Jesu*, 159ff.

54   Mark 14:12–31.

disciples. The most important thing that happened at dinner was the speech Jesus made. Jesus predicted that his disciples would betray him and he told them about the suffering that awaited him. The canonical documents record how Peter attempted to convince him that he would not abandon him, but Jesus predicted how Peter would deny him three times before the rooster crowed.[55] James was surprised by what Jesus said and expressed his regret to hear what Jesus was thinking would happen to him. And before everyone present, James swore: "Not another morsel of bread shall enter my mouth, until I see the Son of Man risen from the dead."[56] He fulfilled his vow, although his period of fasting was short. The promise would be fulfilled, earning a special appearance of the Risen One, which will be discussed in just a moment.

The way Mary conducted herself at the Last Supper would have far-reaching consequences for the future role of women in the Church. When Jesus said, "This is my body and my blood," in reference to a cup of water, Mary smiled a little like she did not entirely believe what he was saying. That was a terrible mistake. Because of that, Jesus forbade older women from serving the Eucharist. Martha complained: "This is Mary's fault. All because she got caught smiling." But Mary apologized, saying that her laughter really meant nothing since Jesus had already determined that women would not serve the Eucharist—"the weaker (i.e., the woman) will be saved by the intervention of the stronger person (i.e., the man)."[57]

With that the evening wound down, and they got up from their meal. Jesus gathered everyone around him and said: "Before I am handed over, let us worship the Father together." He ordered them to form a circle and to hold hands. Jesus stood in the center and told everyone to respond with an "Amen." And he began to sing a hymn:

55   Mark 14:66–72.

56   *(Cop.) Gos. Heb.* 17 (de Santos, 38).

57   *Apostolic Constitutions*, text in von Harnack, *Die Lehre der zwölf*, 28–29. Cited by Bauer, *Das Leben Jesu*, 165.

Glory to You, Father
Glory to You, Grace
Glory to You, Spirit
(And all the disciples responded: *"Amen"*)
We praise you, Father
We thank you, Light
in whom there is no darkness. Amen
I will be saved
and I will be the Savior. Amen.
I will be freed
and I will free. Amen.
I am will eat
and I will be eaten. Amen.
I will hear
and I will be heard. Amen.
I am a mirror
in which you recognize me. Amen.
I am a door
at which you knock. Amen.
You who you dance recognize what I do
for this suffering that I am going to suffer
belongs to you.
There is no way you could
know what you suffer,
had I not been sent by the Father
to you, as the Logos.
What people see in me,
that I am not.
What I am you shall see,
when you come to me.
I jump;
but you, for your part, understand the Whole.
And when you understand, you will say:
'Glory to you, Father.' Amen.[58]

---

58   *Acts John* 94–96.

How can this hymn be explained? At first glance, it is just so strange. And what about the vegetarianism of the Nazarene, revealed so strikingly in a Passover meal with no lamb and no wine, which were essential to observing the special day? The only explanation is found in the secret teachings of Jesus.

The time was nigh when Jesus' life would end in a very tragic way, for all to see, a death brought about by a single act of treachery by one of Jesus' own disciples. But there is one document that tells a totally different story. Most have no idea, but the one who came to be called a traitor was actually quite the opposite. The document begins with the statement that Judas was actually the favorite disciple of Jesus, the one who knew him best, the only one who was capable of receiving his secret teachings. That document opens with these words: "The secret discourse of the revelation that Jesus spoke to Judas Iscariot during eight days prior to the three days before he kept the Passover."[59] Then Jesus promises to Judas: "Remove yourself from the other disciples. I will tell you the mysteries of the kingdom. You can reach them, but you will suffer a lot to get there." Later Jesus added: "Come, and I will teach you about the [secrets] no man has ever seen. For there is a great and limitless realm, the size of which no generation of angels has ever seen. In it is the Great Invisible Spirit."[60]

During those days, Jesus revealed to Judas the secrets of the upper divine world, the lower divine world, and the cosmos, how the first man was created, and the destiny of mankind with the destruction of the wicked. But above all, he made a shocking request. Jesus tasked Judas with handing him over to the Jews, so that the divine plan for the sacrifice of Jesus on the cross for all mankind would be fulfilled. Obviously, Judas would not be handing over Jesus, who is a divine being, just his body. And obviously no one understood any of this, for this reason Judas remains the traitor even to the present day.

---

59   *Gos. Jud.* 33:1ff.

60   *Gos. Jud.* 47:1–10.

Jesus promised to bless what Judas did. The betrayal goes hand-in-hand with the promise of great reward, namely eternal rest and a place of prominence among others there. "Truly I say to you, you shall be greater than all of them, for the person who bears me, you will sacrifice him.[61] "Behold, all things will have been said. Look up and see the cloud and its light and the stars that revolve around it, and the star that is the guide—that is your star." Judas then looked up and saw the luminous cloud, and he entered it.[62]

---

61   *Gos. Jud.* 56:15–20.
62   *Gos. Jud.* 57:15–20.

The Final Days of Jesus

After observing the Passover meal with his disciples, Jesus went with them to the Garden of Gethsemane.[1] It was already Tuesday night heading into early hours of Wednesday, the 12th of Nisan.[2] A number of surprises awaited the disciples. But for Jesus they were anything but surprises. He had already arranged everything with Judas Iscariot, who came with a strong group of men once the darkness had settled in. He was apparently willing to cooperate with the authorities of the people to get rid of their hindrance, especially during the time of the great Feast of Passover when messianic-revolutionary riots were feared most. Part of the people, after the triumphal entry of Jesus into Jerusalem, demanded that the priests, along with the Nazarene, stand up to the Romans and finally shake off the foreign yoke that had enslaved the land of Yahweh. But the Jerusalem clergy knew all too well the impossibility of this plan, and they were not willing to lose the benefits of their collusion with the Romans. Even more, they did not like the idea of losing all of their possessions should such a plan fail.[3]

But the people were wrong when Judas showed up leading a treacherous and cunning operation. Things were not as they seemed. Judas was the instrument of divine wisdom to arouse the

1 Mark 14:31–42.
2 (Syr.) Did. Apost. 31.
3 Cf. the Slavic version of Flavius Josephus' Bellum Judaicum for an amplified discussion: Berendts (ed.), Die Zeugnisse vom Christentum im slavischen. See specifically pp. 9ff. and 48ff.

hatred of the Demiurge[4] against Jesus, bringing the life of Jesus to a dramatic end—and through it redemption. It was not impossible that the humanity of Jesus, that is his body, would decay prior to the hard role it played in the final moments of Jesus' life. Jesus had to prevent this possibility, and, for this reason, the apparent betrayal of Judas fulfilled a helpful mission with his alleged felony by bringing about the inevitable passion of the Savior. Some later Gnostics stumbled upon this detail, and they were very grateful for it.[5]

According to the ancient records, Jesus' arrest, trial before Pilate and Herod, flogging, and walk to Golgotha all occurred from Wednesday the 13th to Friday the 15th of Nisan[6]—and the canonical documents are not misleading in this regard.[7] In addition to what is found in the canonical Gospels, there are some accounts preserved in other sources that are worth considering here. Both Simon Peter and Nicodemus made up some interesting stories about what happened on these particular days of Jesus' life, especially the final day. There was a man named Ananias, an officer in the praetorian guard in the seventeenth year of the reign of Theodosius and sixth of Valentinian (AD 424–425), who started to keep track of the reports concerning Jesus that some Jews had left on file with Pontius Pilate. Luckily, he found one of these documents, called the Acts of Pilate or the *Gospel of Nicodemus*, of which the first part deals with Jesus' passion. The text, it is said, had been written by Nicodemus in Hebrew and then delivered to the chief priests as a testimony. It was later translated into Greek and preserved to the present day.

This manuscript includes information about a meeting that took place on Monday the 10th of Nisan[8] among the chief

---

4   See the last chapter dealing with the "secret teachings" of Jesus.
5   *Gospel of Judas*, cited by Irenaeus (*Against Heresies* 1:31:1) and Epiphanius (*Panarion* 38:1, 3).
6   (Syr.) Did. Apost. 31.
7   Mark 14–15 and parallel passages.
8   (Syr.) Did. Apost. 31.

priests, Annas and Caiaphas, Gamaliel, Levi, Alexander, the more renowned scribes, and some of the more prominent Jewish figures, who were not part of the Sanhedrin.[9] They appeared before Pilate, accusing Jesus of many different crimes. The governor had mixed feelings. On the one hand, Jesus was a dangerous figure; a messianic movement represented a huge threat to the security of Rome. On the other hand, Pilate had heard good things about Jesus, yet his opponents were saying the complete opposite. For a Roman, all this religious fanaticism and the contempt they showed for everything foreign was incomprehensible, as if they were better than everyone else. But as prosecutor, he had no choice but to receive them, though with great reluctance. When everyone assembled and the room became quite like a courtroom, Pilate walked in and sat down. Then, the spokesman of the Jews, Caiaphas, said to the Roman: "We have brought you a very dangerous individual, who needs your immediate attention. We know that this Jesus, who we have arrested, is the son of a carpenter from Galilee, though he calls himself a messiah and king. He violates the Sabbath and seeks to abolish the law of our forefathers." "What specific things has he done?" asked Pilate. One of the priests answered: "We have a law prohibiting a person from healing on the Sabbath, but this man, using trickery, has healed the blind and disabled. In some cases, he mixed dirt with his saliva, which is prohibited on the Sabbath because it constitutes work. Also, he casts out demons through an alliance with Beelzebub." Pilate answered: "Sounds more like an alliance with Aesculapius." "We do not know," continued the priests, "but bring the evildoer to appear before you."

Pilate agreed to their request, although reluctantly, and he sent a young messenger to bring Jesus to him. The boy led Jesus to the threshold of the courtroom. When they arrived, he took off his coat, as a sign of respect for Jesus, and laid it on the ground, on which Jesus stepped as he entered the assembly. The Jews were outraged, preventing the boy from passing, and cried out: "What is this boy doing, laying his cloak on the floor and allowing Jesus

9   Cf. Bauer, *Das Leben Jesu*, 187.

to walk on it like he is some sort of king?" The messenger, with Pilate's permission, responded: "Governor, when you sent me from Jerusalem to Alexander, I witnessed something remarkable. I saw this man coming in through the gates of the city riding on a donkey, and all the people were cheering for him.[10] He must be someone important." One of the Jewish men responded: "What do you know what people cheering? It would have been in Hebrew anyways, and you only know Greek!" The boy responded back: "Well, I asked someone there, and they translated it for me." Pilate then intervened: "Tell me, then, what were these people shouting?" The priests were somewhat embarrassed, but after a moment one of them said: "Hosanna to the Son of David." Pilate then said: "If you yourselves bear witness to what the people were shouting, why are you then criticizing my messenger?" And turning to the boy, he ordered them: "Let him pass."

And when Jesus entered the room, the flag bearers bowed, as if moved by an invisible force, and lowered their flags. The Jews cried out again in sharp protest. It was as if the flag bearers were worshiping Jesus. This time Pilate was in agreement, saying to his men: "This is going to cost you. Why have you done such a thing?" And one of them said: "We are Greeks and worshipers of the gods. Why should we lower our flags in adoration of this man? We were just holding the flags. The flags lowered themselves. We had nothing to do with it."

Pilate, in order to test what the flag bearer had said, told Caiaphas: "Choose twelve strong men from among you and let them hold the flags. And at the same time he ordered the young messenger to take Jesus back outside. After a few moments of confusion, while the strongest twelve men were being selected, they prepared to receive Jesus again. Meanwhile, other people had gathered in the court, including some supporters of Jesus. Pilate urged those holding the flags with these words: "I swear by Caesar that whoever lowers his flag before this Jew shall have his head cut off." So, he ordered that Jesus return to the room. When he did,

---

10   Mark 11:1–11.

the flags were lowered, honoring the presence of Jesus. It was at that point that Pilate began to fear the defendant from Galilee. In fact, he was close to calling off the whole tribunal and leaving.

Pilate received a message, written on a tablet, from his wife Procula about Jesus. Pilate read the message and told the priests: "You know that my wife is a pious woman and she always takes your advice in matters of religion. She tends to follow your ways more so than mine." They replied: "We know." Pilate said: "Well, my wife just sent me this message: 'Have nothing to do with that righteous man, for last night I suffered greatly in a dream because of him.'"[11] (Procula did not know it at the time, but her act of piety towards Jesus would lead to the healing of the strong pains that plagued her.)[12]

The priests responded to Procula's message, saying to Pilate: "Have we not told you that he is a wizard? He has surely sent a dream to your wife." Pilate asked Jesus: "Are you going to say nothing about the testimony of the priests against you?" Jesus then responded: "Each man's mouth is his own, and they can speak good and evil. They will see." "What are we going to see?" some of the accusers cried out in outrage. "You are a child born out of fornication who ran away to Egypt and learned magic."

At that moment there erupted a tremendous altercation between the priests and some of Jesus' sympathizers, who came to his defense before the governor. They argued that Jesus was not an illegitimate child. He was someone who did good for others, and he performed miracles and healed people.[13] Some were accusing them, including Jesus, without a shred of evidence of course, of robbing the temple with some of his supporters and taking the

11   Matt 27:19.

12   Cf. the Slavic version of Flavius Josephus' *Bellum Judaicum* for an amplified discussion: Berendts (ed.), *Die Zeugnisse vom Christentum im slavischen*. See specifically pp. 9ff. and 48ff.

13   Cf. *Acts Pet. Paul* 40–42: *Report of Pilate to Emperor Claudius*, in Lipsius-Bonnet (ed.), *Acta Apostalorum Apocrypha*, I 196ff.; it lists the miracles of Jesus, taken from the canonical Gospels.

books of the Law.[14] Pilate simply did not know what to think of all the confusion, but given the dissension among the Jews, he could see that the case was far from settled. And Roman law dictated that "when in doubt, rule in favor of the accused." So, he addressed the priests, somewhat perturbed, and said: "I find no fault in this man deserving of death."

Some time passed between arguments before the court.[15] Herod Antipas the Tetrarch showed up at the palace to take part in the proceedings. The monarch egged Jesus' opponents on and strongly agreed with them that the problem from Galilee should be extinguished, just as he had done with Jesus' cousin, John the Baptist, thus eradicating the beginnings of a possible revolutionary movement. Again, this time in the presence of the Tetrarch, Pilate said he could find in Jesus no fault worthy of death. But Herod was not convinced. Bored and not wanting to antagonize the leaders of the Jews who had bribed him with plenty of money,[16] Pilate washed his hands in public, exonerating himself from any guilt in the death of a just man. And he said to Herod: "You take him and punish him as you wish. But I can see some in the crowd here who in no way agree with any of this." The priests shouted: "For this we have all assembled, to see Jesus put to death, because he has proclaimed himself the son of God and the king of Israel."[17]

With Pilate having washed his hands of everything, King Herod, who was instigated by Caiaphas,[18] took full responsibility over the trial and the sentencing. And Herod delivered Jesus over to the Jewish crowd with these words: "Do to this man exactly what I told you to do."[19]

---

14   *Jos. of Arim.* 1:3–2:4.

15   Matt 27:11–27 and parallel passages.

16   Cf. the Slavic version of Flavius Josephus' *Bellum Judaicum* for an amplified discussion: Berendts (ed.), *Die Zeugnisse vom Christentum im slavischen.* See specifically pp. 9ff. and 48ff.

17   *Acts Pil.* 2–5.

18   *Act Verc.* 8.

19   *Gos. Pet.* 1:2; *Acts Andr. Matt.* 26; *Ascen. Isa.* 11:19.

Herod was about to dismiss the assembly when Nicodemus, a qualified Pharisee and secret friend of Jesus, took courage and addressed Pilate in the presence of everyone: "I beg you, prosecutor, kind as you are, permit me to say a few words." Pilate gave him permission, and Nicodemus spoke thus: "What do you intend to do with this man? Do you not agree that he has done many miracles? Release him and do him no harm. If the miracles come from God, they will stand; but if they are the works of man, they will not last. Also Moses, when he was sent by God to the Egyptians, did many miracles in the presence of Pharaoh. You know that there were others, like Jannes and Jambres, who tried perform the same miracles, but eventually they perished, as well as those who gave them credit."[20]

Hearing this, most of the Jews became even more furious and began to grind their teeth against Nicodemus: "You have become his disciple. That is why you are saying such nonsense. You can have the truth of the Nazarene and your share in the world to come. But, as for us, we want nothing to do with him."[21]

And with these words the majority of the people were going to head home to prepare for the feast—except for a few, who stayed with Jesus, and some soldiers—and that is when Pilate had the idea of letting the people choose between Jesus and Barabbas, offering to pardon one of the two men in honor of the Passover. The canonical Gospels detail what happened next. Barabbas was freed[22] and Jesus was condemned to die on the cross, accompanied by Dimas and Gestas, two known zealots of the Law who had rebelled against the Romans and their allies. Gestas was a really evil man. He used to kill travelers with his sword, while he left others naked. He used to hang women from trees by their feet and then cut off their breasts. He also preferred to drink the blood of children, children of his enemies. The second man, Dimas, was

---

20   Cf. Acts 5:35–39.

21   *Acts Pil.* 5.

22   Matt 27:15ff.

from Galilee and owned an inn. He was different than Gestas. Dimas wanted to rob from the rich and give to the poor.[23]

Once Barabbas was freed and Jesus was sentenced, the latter was scourged and mocked with a crown of thorns. According to the sources,[24] the Roman soldiers had little participation in these events. These cruel acts were carried out mostly by Jews.

The Jews took Jesus and the two thieves and drove them out of the gates of the city,[25] and there they crucified them. And it was the Jews, not Pilate, who placed a sign on the cross that read: "King of Israel."[26] Throughout the whole ordeal—the hammer driving the nails into Jesus all the way to raising the cross with his body affixed—Jesus uttered not a word, nor did he feel any pain.[27] The thief on the left, writhing in unimaginable pain, insulted Jesus for his apparent impotence: "How do they call you son of God? If you cannot help yourself, how is it that you will be able to help anyone else? Even if our paths had crossed before today and I knew you were a king, I would not have anything to do with you."

Dimas, though, was sorrowful and repentant of his past life. He addressed Jesus, saying: "Please forgive me for the sins I have committed! Do not let the stars come against me in my judgment or the moon when you go to judge me, because all that I did that was evil I did so at night. Do not move the sun, which is now turning dark for you, so that you can reveal the evils of my heart." Jesus gently replied: "In truth I tell you, Dimas, today you shall be with me in paradise. But the sons of the kingdom will be left out in the outer darkness."[28]

The Jews who were standing nearby heard the exchange and were angry with the thief. They ordered that his legs not be

---

23 *Jos. of Arim.* 1:2.

24 *Gos. Pet.* 6–9.

25 Other sources, such as the *Acts of John* 97 and the *Ascension of Isaiah* 11:20, indicate that the crucifixion took place inside the city.

26 *Gos. Pet.* 11.

27 *Gos. Pet.* 10.

28 *Jos. of Arim.* 3:1–4.

broken, which would have accelerated his death, thus prolonging his suffering.[29] But a soldier named Longinus pierced Jesus' side with a spear, and water and blood flowed in abundance from the wound.[30]

It was now noon, and a terrible darkness came over all Judea. Stars were seen in the dark sky above, but they did not shine; in the corner of the sky was the moon, dipped in blood. The rumble of thunder was heard in the distance, and the hearts of the people shrank in their chests, while Golgotha shook violently and the ground split in two.[31]

While these things were taking place on the outskirts of Jerusalem, John, the beloved disciple, had taken refuge in a cave that was on the Mount of Olives. He wept for all that had transpired. Suddenly, while Jesus was still suffering his final moments, the cave lit up and the Master gloriously appeared to him. He said: "John, because of those men down there I am being crucified. They have pierced me with a spear, beat me with reeds, and soon they will give me gall to drink. But I need to talk to you. Listen carefully to my words, because I want to tell you some important things. I am the one who brought you here to this mountain, so that you will hear what a disciple should learn from his teacher."

Then Jesus showed John a luminous cross, and next to it was a large crowd without any form. Jesus was crucified on the cross, though without form. All John perceived was a voice—a sweet, kind, and truly divine voice, which was the same voice of the one who spoke to him in the cave. The voice said: "John, one thing you need to hear: Do you see this luminous cross? For you he shall be called Word, Reason, Door, Way, Bread, Seed; sometimes he will be called Son; other times, Father, Spirit, Life, or Truth and Grace. By these names he will be known among men. This

---

29 *Gos. Pet.* 14.

30 *Acts Pil.* 16:7.

31 *Anaph. Pil.* 7: *Doctrine of Addai* (G. Phillips [ed., trans.], *The Doctrine of Addai*, 27, cited by Bauer, *Das Leben Jesu*, 226); *T. 12 Patr.*, *T. Levi* 4; *Sib. Or.* VIII 306; I 375.

luminous cross is the truth, and it represents the Limit of harmony and wisdom with respect to that which is outside the Fullness."

Jesus stopped for a moment to see if John understood and before continuing: "This cross is the Limit of all things and gives stability to that which is unstable. The real cross is not the wood that you will see taken down from this mountain. Nor am I in that wood; I am the voice that you now hear. People have me for what I am not. Just as the heavenly Rest cannot be explained, nor can I, the Lord of that Rest, be explained. The formless crowd that you see surrounding the cross is the lower nature. But when some of them draw near and hear my voice, it will not be as it is now, but what I am. When you listen to me, I will again be what it was, because from me you what you are. Do not worry about the crowd, but despise those who are outside the mystery."

John was absolutely silent and remained focused on the words of the Revealer, which could only be understood by meditating alone on their depth. There was another short pause. Then the luminous voice continued talking and concluded his speech with these words: "Actually, I have not suffered what the people have said I suffered. My whole passion is a mystery. I have been through it and I have not been through it. I have hung on a cross yet I have not hung. My blood has been shed, yet it has not been shed. In a word, what the people say I have suffered is not the truth. I suffered precisely what they do not say. I alone know who I am. Others do not know. I have mine, but yours, look at it in me and understand it in me and my words. Understand the Logos and you will understand the Lord, and thirdly, you will understand the Man and what he has suffered."

And then the radiant Jesus disappeared, and John saw him taken up to heaven. John was comforted by these words, and he decided to return to Golgotha. While he was going down, though, he smiled with contempt at the people, who stood around the wooden cross and were not able to understand the profundity of what was taking place on that hill.

Meanwhile, as it grew darker and darker, the Jews began to worry. They were afraid that the sun might set before the crucified had breathed their last breaths. That would have violated their Law and rendered the feast impure, just as it is written: "If a man has committed a sin deserving of death and he is put to death, and you hang him on a tree, his corpse shall not hang all night on the tree."[32] One of those present said: "Give the Nazarene gall to drink with vinegar. This drink is poisonous and will hasten his death."

They prepared the drink and gave it to Jesus, who drank from it. Some of those present, overwhelmed by the darkness, had sent their servants into the city to fetch torches. There was a great silence, so that all could hear. Jesus raised his voice and said: "My Strength, my Strength, you have abandoned me."[33]

And when he had said these words, he gave up his spirit. At that very moment the temple veil was ripped in two,[34] and the architrave of the main entrance shook and came crashing down.[35] Joseph of Arimathea was not with Jesus at the cross but had come to the palace to request a meeting with Pilate. He asked one of the guards to announce him. Joseph was a friend, both of Jesus and Pilate.[36] The towering palace was eerily silent compared to all the uproar that took place just a few hours prior. Pilate received Joseph, who begged him not to leave the body of Jesus in the hands of his enemies. Joseph himself offered to take him down from the cross and bury him in a tomb carved into the rock he had prepared for himself in a garden, called the "Garden of Joseph"[37] near Jerusalem. Pilate gave him permission to do so, and Joseph went on his way.

---

32   Deut 21:22–23a.

33   *Gos. Pet.* 15–19.

34   Matt 27:51ff.

35   *Gos. Naz.* (de Santos, p. 41, n. 27); *Testaments of the Twelve Patriarchs, Testimony of Benjamin.* This was a sign that God had abandoned the temple and the Spirit was given to the Jews.

36   *Gos. Pet.* 3.

37   *Gos. Pet.* 24.

They took the body of Jesus down from the cross with great care, taking notice that, to their surprise, the body of the thief on his right was gone. It was dark, so they thought that might be why they could not see the body. However, the body of the thief on the left was there and it looked horrible, almost like a dragon.[38] They removed the nails from Jesus' body and prepared to carry it to the tomb. Again, the whole earth shook and trembled, causing the Jews to panic big time.[39] When they carried Jesus down from Golgotha, the sun began to shine again, and they realized it was still six in the afternoon. Joseph, being helped by the women, carefully took Jesus' body to a wagon that he had prepared close by. Then they drove it to his garden. Once there, they washed Jesus' body,[40] wrapped it in a shroud, and laid the body in the tomb.

Some of the Jews, even some of the elders and priests, began to realize the evil they had brought upon themselves and began to beat their chests out of regret for what they had done. Some thought that what happened could prove costly to Jerusalem and that punishment was imminent.[41] Later, after Pentecost, these individuals would join the ranks of the first disciples. Peter, meanwhile, along with the other followers of Jesus, was engulfed in sorrow, and had taken to hiding out of fear for the Jews. The order had gone out that all the disciples should be arrested as evildoers and enemies of the temple.[42]

Most of the Pharisees, scribes, priests, and elders, when they heard that some of the people had cried out and beat their breasts as a sign of repentance, became fearful that there might be some trouble on the horizon. So, they went to Pilate for help. He told them: "My wife and I have spent all day without food or drink,

---

38   *Jos. of Arim.* 4:1.

39   *Gos. Pet.* 21.

40   *Gos. Pet.* 24.

41   *Doctrine of Addai* (G. Phillips [ed., trans.], *The Doctrine of Addai*, 27, cited by Bauer, *Das Leben Jesu*, 235).

42   *Gos. Pet.* 26.

saddened by all that has transpired. Tell me, how do you explain the darkness that came over the land?" They replied: "It was just a solar eclipse, as usual. Do not worry about that.[43] Do not let such an unimportant figure cause you any concern. But we ask that you will give us enough soldiers to guard the tomb of the Galilean for at least three days, lest his disciples attempt to steal his body. If they succeeded in doing so, the last deception would be worse than the first."

Pilate gave them what they wanted and ordered the commander Petronius, a centurion, and some additional soldiers to stand guard around the tomb. They put seven seals on the rock of the tomb. And after they set up camp, they took turns keeping watch, the soldiers in groups of two, as well as some Jews from Jerusalem.[44] Meanwhile, some other Jews, hearing that it was Joseph who had asked Pilate for the body of Jesus, were enraged and went to his home, snatched him off his bed, and threw him in jail.[45] They told him: "You know how late it is, Saturday is upon us, and there is nothing we can do to you. But come the first of the week, you will surely die. Your body will never see that tomb, for the birds of the air shall feast on your corpse."[46]

There was no window in Joseph's cell. The Jews locked him in tight and placed guards outside and returned to their homes to observe the Sabbath.

---

43 *Acts Pil.* 11:1–2.
44 *Gos. Pet.* 30–33.
45 *Jos. of Arim.* 4:1; *Acts Pil.* 12:1.
46 *Acts Pil.* 12:1.

The Descent into Hell

On the first day of the week, close to dawn, the priests and members of the Sanhedrin gathered in the synagogue to discuss what they should do with Joseph. After a little while, the council decided almost unanimously to put him to death, although there were differences on exactly how Joseph would die. For the time being, they decided to take Joseph out of his cell and force him to testify against Jesus' other friends, who they wanted put to death as well. Some officers came to the house that served as a jail and opened the door. But, lo and behold, he was not there! The seals were intact, the guards had not seen anything really out of the ordinary, and Caiaphas was in possession of the key the entire night. The officers returned to the chamber of the Sanhedrin, completely astonished, and reported what they had found. Everything seemed to be in order, but it was as if Joseph had vanished out of thin air. Everyone was amazed and marveled. Things calmed down, and they thought otherwise about taking action against the followers of Jesus.

While they were all still assembled, in rushed some guards, including one of Caiaphas' personal servants,[1] who had been guarding the tomb where Jesus lay. They were shouting: "Jesus has risen! Jesus has risen!"

The Sanhedrin could not believe what they were hearing. They crowded around the messengers and began to question them. They were gasping for breath and trying to calm themselves down

---

1   (Cop.) Gos. Heb. 17 (de Santos, 38).

as they told everyone what had taken place:[2] "It was nighttime[3] and dawn was still a ways away. Suddenly, we thought we heard a loud voice from heaven. The earth began to shake. The ground literally shook under our feet, and we saw the heavens opened. The sky shone with a brightness seven times brighter than when the sun is at its peak during the day.[4] What looked like two men descended from above in the middle of all the brightness. They were beaming white, their appearance like snow and lightening. And they went up to the tomb. And as fast as thunder thunders in a summer storm, these men appeared before our very eyes. The stone that the friends of the Nazarene had rolled over the entrance was rolled away, but it was like it rolled itself away.[5] The tomb was opened, and two men went inside. There was also a huge fissure in the ground, so deep that it revealed the foundations of the earth."[6]

Someone in the audience asked: "Why did you not seize these two men?" One of the messengers answered: "We were scared to death. We thought we were going to die, that we would never see the light of day. Seriously, how were we going to seize them? The soldiers who were standing guard saw everything too. They ran away and woke up the centurion and the elders that were keeping watch with us. I know it sounds crazy, but they had not woken up yet. The soldiers were explaining everything to their commander and while they were doing so, we all saw[7] three men walking out of the tomb. Two of them were helping the other as they left, and we also saw a cross that was walking by itself, like it had feet, following after the three. The head of the first two reached to heaven, and that of the third surpassed even theirs. The body of the third was glorious too, but it was different from the other two.

---

2   *Acts Pil.* 13; *Gos. Pet.* 35ff.

3   *Gos. Pet.* 35, 45.

4   *Anaph. Pil.* 9.

5   *Gos. Pet.* 37.

6   *Anaph. Pil.* 9.

7   *Report of Pilate to Emperor Claudius*, in Lipsius-Bonnet (ed.), *Acta Apostalorum Apocrypha* (1891), I 136,19–138,2.

The third man handed his shroud to the servant of Caiaphas,[8] but it immediately flew out of his hand. And again, we heard a voice from heaven, saying: 'Have you preached to them that sleep?' It sounded like the cross answered and said: 'Yes.' We all thought it was the cross. It sounds crazy that we would say a piece of wood was speaking, I know. And now here we are. We ran here to share the news with you all, and Pilate's soldiers ran to tell him."

The members of the Sanhedrin decided to get over to Pilate's palace as quickly as possible to discuss the strange news about the tomb where Jesus' body had been placed. When they arrived at the palace, the soldiers were still reporting to Pilate what they had seen. Some of the pagans said: "Truly this man was the son of God."[9] The priests arrived just in time to hear that exclamation. The Roman governor voiced his anger at the Jews, saying: "You all did this! I am innocent of this man's blood."[10]

The priests and other members of the Sanhedrin were silent. All they did was motion with their hands for Pilate to send the soldiers out of the room. Once they were alone, the Jews talked with Pilate and offered him a substantial amount of money as a bribe for him to order the centurion and the soldiers to keep what they had seen secret, threatening them with death if they did not. If anyone asked about the empty tomb, the Jews said they should just say that the disciples had stolen the body.[11] And the Jews paid the soldiers to keep their mouths shut as well.

And so the meeting came to a close. The next day, a priest and doctor of the Law called Phinehas, whose name was Adas, and a Levite named Haggai came down from Galilee to Jerusalem. They went straight to the Sanhedrin and reported to everyone present: "We just came from Galilee and have seen Jesus sitting on the mount named Mamilch with his disciples. He was instructing them. He has commanded them to go into all the world and preach

8   (Cop.) Gos. Heb. 17 (de Santos, 38).
9   Mark 15:39.
10   Luke 23:22.
11   Gos. Pet. 43–49.

his message." One of the members urged them with an agitated tone: "Swear to the God of Israel that you have truly heard and seen what you just said." "As surely as God lives," he replied, "I promise before the God of our fathers that we heard and saw these things." The high priest asked: "Did you come here to tell us this or to fulfill a vow of some sort?" "To fulfill a vow," they replied. "If you have come to fulfill a vow to God," continued Caiaphas, "then what is all this nonsense for?"

The men from Galilee insisted over again and again that everything was true. One of the priests took a book of the Law and made them swear not to say anything to anyone, so they would not scare the people. Then they gave them food and drink and selected three men to accompany them on their journey back to Galilee. The truth is, though, these men were really sent to spy and make sure the men were going to stay quiet. When they were alone, the priests and other members of the Sanhedrin kept arguing about all the reports they were hearing. They said to one another: "It is one thing to say that his disciples stole his body, but how can his soul be walking around Galilee?" And while they were asking themselves questions like these, one of them made the following proposal to the assembly: "In times past it has happened, as we can see in the Scriptures, that someone has been taken away by the Spirit and later left by a mountain. This happened, for example, with Elijah. Why not organize an expedition and go look for this Jesus?"

Everyone liked the idea, so they sent some people to search throughout Judea and Galilee. They did not find Jesus. They only found some of his disciples and Joseph of Arimathea. The envoy knew that Joseph had escaped from prison, but they did not lay a finger on him. They approached him and said in a friendly tone: "Peace to you, Joseph."

Joseph was reluctant to talk with the men who had been sent by his real enemies, but he stopped for just a moment so as not to be rude. The envoy from the Sanhedrin was convinced that something extraordinary had happened to Joseph, so they were nice to him and tried to get him to share how he had escaped from prison. After begging him, Joseph finally conceded. This is the story Joseph told them:[12]

It was the first day of the week. I was tired of sitting on the floor, so I stood up to pray. Suddenly, there was a super bright light that lit up the dark room where I was locked up. At that moment, it felt like the whole house was lifted up into the air from corner to corner. The walls were taken away and nothing prevented me from leaving. But I fell to the ground, afraid of whatever was happening. Someone grabbed my hand and pulled me up. Then I realized someone else was there, also bright but not as bright. At first, I saw only a bright body and did not know who it was that pulled me up from the ground. I could smell something like a scented ointment. It was so strong that it penetrated to the inside of my body. When I blinked my eyes, it seemed like I was in another world. One said to me: "Fear not, Joseph, open your eyes and behold the one who is speaking to you." A feeling of great peace came over me. I was not sure what I saw, but fearing that the appearance might be a ghost, I began to recite aloud the commandments prescribed by our Law. It is well known that if a ghost appears, reciting a portion of the Law, especially the Decalogue, will surely protect you. But the radiant figure remained with me. It looked like some sort of angel of light, though I cannot describe exactly how it looked. His flesh was not like ordinary man, but a perfect flesh.[13] After a short moment of doubt, I guessed who it might be.

I said: "Master Elijah, are you here to accompany my soul for the last trip?" But he replied: "I am not Elijah. I am Jesus, the one you buried."

---

12 *Jos. of Arim.* 4:1ff.; *Acts Pil.* 15:6ff.
13 *Soph. Jes. Chr.*, *Biblioteca de Nag Hammadi* III 4, 91,18.

Then I opened my eyes, and I could see his glorious body. Indeed, he had the same shape as when he lived among us, but the whole aspect of his flesh was different—ethereal, radiant, light, pure, and perfect. It was similar to what some of his favorite disciples had reported about how Jesus had shown himself at the time of his transfiguration on the mount.[14] Really, he looked like a large, bright angel, but way more amazing. I just cannot describe it.[15] The one who was with him whispered to me: "I am Dimas, who was crucified next to Jesus and now I follow him."

And seeing him with his transformed body, simple and majestic all at once, I fell to my knees, took his hand, and kissed it. But he picked me up and gently encouraged me: "This joy awaits all those who are faithful to Jesus."

Joseph paused to observe the reaction of the envoy. Then, after a moment, he continued his story:

Then I heard a voice like that of a large crowd, saying, "He who was the thief has already arrived in paradise, for which he was prepared. We have been appointed to serve until the great day comes, when the saints will enter the heavenly Jerusalem in triumph." And the men who had pulled me out of jail took me by the hand and led me to my house. When I arrived I could see Jesus no more, nor his companion. And now I simply cannot wait to see them again.

Joseph of Arimathea uttered these last words and then became silent, waiting for the reaction of those who had questioned him. But the envoy was really fascinated by the story and, the truth is, they did not know what to say. They deliberated among themselves and arrived at a decision. Though they had not found Jesus, they

14   Mark 9:1ff.

15   *Soph. Jes. Chr., Biblioteca de Nag Hammadi* III 4, 90,14–91,20.

did have a really good story to report, so they decided to return to Jerusalem and tell the priests what had happened.

And so the envoy did. Everyone said goodbye to Joseph, bidding him farewell with a kiss of peace, and off they went to the capital. But another surprise awaited them. Something else happened before they could get to Jerusalem and share with Annas and Caiaphas and the rest of the Sanhedrin all that Joseph had told them. Some residents of Arimathea went to Jerusalem to confirm, with respect to their city, what had already been reported earlier in Jerusalem and elsewhere, namely that on the first day of the week, right when the disciples of the Nazarene claimed that Jesus had been resurrected, some tombs had opened and some had come out, alive, thanking God, and praising Jesus. None of the members of the Sanhedrin believed those reports when they first heard them. For them, it was all just more ridiculousness, fantasies of the fanatical followers of the Nazarene. The people from Arimathea arrived in Jerusalem the same day as the envoy, that went looking for Jesus in Galilee. They appeared before the Sanhedrin with news of an unusual event. Two of Simeon's sons came out of their graves and walked about Arimathea. Simeon was an old teacher, the same man who, according to the disciples, held Jesus in his arms when he was presented in the temple.[16] Their names were Leucio and Carino, and they told extraordinary stories of what they witnessed between the time Jesus had been put to death and the time was raised. It was all quite the surprise since, supposedly, Jesus' body had been locked away behind a large stone in the garden of Joseph. One of the men from Arimathea told the Sanhedrin: "Those two men, Leucio and Carino, who had been laid in the ground not long ago, have risen with the Nazarene. Their tombs are now open and empty. They are very much alive. As we speak, they are walking around Arimathea with renewed bodies."

Given the enormity of this news, the council of elders sent a couple of servants to check and see if there was any truth in it. They

16   Luke 2:25–32.

soon returned and reported that the graves were indeed open. Not only were they open, but they were empty as well. The servants had not seen Leucio or Carino, but people in the city testified that they were alive with renewed bodies. Others claimed to have seen a great crowd, over twelve thousand people, assembling around a nearby mountain, guided by an angel, singing and chanting hymns.[17] The council was shocked to hear such news and gossip. They said: "Let us go to Arimathea ourselves and see if we can find them and question them personally."

Annas, Caiaphas, and a few others left on their mules headed to the town of Arimathea. They managed to find the two brothers after asking a few questions in town. They hugged Leucio and Carino and begged the brothers to tell them everything about their experience in the other world and their return to the present. Leucio and Carino were not very willing to talk, as if their after-death experiences were under the Discipline of the Arcane. They were free to speak, though, because Jesus had given them permission to share the news with a few chosen people.[18] Therefore, after begging and asserting the full authority of the papacy, Annas and Caiaphas were able to persuade Leucio and Carino to return with the chief priests to Jerusalem, where behind closed doors they could explain everything that had taken place.

They all returned to the council chamber. Not a single person was absent. Everyone wanted to hear the story that was about to be told. They gathered in the room and locked the door. They placed a copy of the Book of the Law in the center of the room and made Leucio and Carino take an oath: "We want you to swear by the God of Israel that you are going to tell the truth, and that you will tell us exactly how you were raised from the dead, who brought you back to life, and what you have seen in the other world." The two brothers repeated the oath, made the sign of the cross on their faces, and then told the priests: "Not only are we going to tell you about it, but please, bring us what we need to write, and we will

17   *Descent into Hell*, recension B, 6.
18   *Descent into Hell*, recension B, 2.

write it all down for you too." So, they brought all the materials, and one of the brothers, sitting down, began to relate what had happened to them, while the other wrote in his own hand the words that were said:[19] "Jesus, give us grace to write down all you have wrought in hell while your body still lay the grave!"[20] And with this invocation they proceeded to tell their story:[21]

> We were in Sheol,[22] in the company of all the souls of the dead from since the very beginning of time. You have to know that this place is under the earth. It is dark and gloomy, and it has many compartments. In one section are kept the souls of the damned, for whom there is no hope—casters of spells, magicians, enchanters, blasphemers, those who committed suicide, murderers, the envious, perjurers, slanderers, and other kinds of evil.[23] There they are tortured in many ways, undergoing some of the greatest torments imaginable, hoping and waiting for the final judgment. In another section are the souls of the righteous since Adam that are waiting for the fullness of time to be rescued by the Savior. At some point—it is difficult to say when since there is neither day nor night in this dark and sad place—the room where we were lit up so that we could clearly see each other. The patriarchs and prophets, who had a special relationship with God during their lives, thought about what was about to take place. And the

19   Part II of the *Gospel of Nicodemus* (or, the *Desc. Chr. ad. Inf.*) 1:3ff.; *Gos. Bart.* (Sabbath Codex) 1:6ff.

20   *Sib. Or.* VIII 310–312; *T. Benj.* 9; *Ascen. Isa.* 4:10; 11:19.

21   Part of what these brothers reported is confirmed by an independent account, that of the apostle Bartholomew (*Gos. Bart.* 1:1). It is reported that he also wrote a story at the end of his life with Jesus' answers to questions about various "mysteries of heaven."

22   "Sheol" is the Hebrew designation for the resting place of the souls of the dead. It corresponds to "Hell," but without the sense of punishment.

23   *Gos. Bart.* 4:42.

rest just speculated, not really sure about what was going to transpire.

The prophet Isaiah cried out with joy: "Now is the fulfillment of that of which I prophesied: 'The people who walk in darkness will see a great light.'"[24]

John the Baptist was there too, and he told us all: "Now is the time for salvation to be preached to the dead. If you who have not been cleansed from all your sins, then you should believe in the message that is about to be preached to you. With this message and the baptism of life comes the remission of sins.[25] Believe and you will be free of any blemish."

Adam, when he heard John's exhortation, turned to his son Seth and said: "I want you to tell everyone what happened to us that one time when I was on the brink of death. Everyone, listen, because it has everything to do with what is happening right now." Seth spoke up, addressing everyone in a solemn tone: "As my father said, he came close to dying one time. He sent me to the door of paradise hoping that I might procure, with the help of an angel, a special oil from a wonderful tree, which could heal my father. I went to the door and began to pray. I found an angel, who asked me: 'What are you seeking, Seth? Are you looking for the oil from the wonderful tree that heals the sick? You will not find it right now. Go and tell your father that one will descend upon the earth five thousand years after the creation of the world, and this one will heal the souls and all diseases. It is with this oil that he needs to be anointed, but for now it is impossible.' Behold, now is the time of which this angel spoke."

And hearing the news, all of the righteous in Sheol shouted with joy. But Satan, the prince of darkness, came

---

24   Isa 9:2.
25   *Ep. Apost.* 27.

and spoke to Hell (which is the name of the guardian of Sheol): "Hey you, insatiable devourer of all. There is a certain Jew out there named Jesus who showed special powers during his life. His disciples are saying that he is the son of God, but he is not. I know he is a mere man, because I heard him say, 'My soul is sorrowful even unto death.' The truth is that he has caused me enough trouble in life, but I managed to turn a whole multitude of Jews against him. They put him to death. But now we shall give a definitive account of who he is."

Hell replied with some trepidation: "Satan, if this is a man who dealt you several blows during his life, then how are we going to deal with him now?" "Do not be afraid," Satan answered. "I rallied the Jews against him and they crucified him, killing him. Get ready to stand firm in your dwelling."

"Slanderer, son of perdition," Hell said, "you must be kidding me. I recently devoured a man named Lazarus, but this Jesus ripped him out of my bowels with only a single word. I fear that, if he enters my domain, he will set free all those I have devoured from the beginning to the end, snatching them all away. And then he will take them someplace else."

Satan and Hell continued talking, when all of a sudden there was a loud bang. A loud voice rang throughout the unfathomable space of hell: "Lift up your gates, O princes. Rise, O eternal doors! The king of glory will now enter."[26] Satan began to tremble, as Hell awaited the entrance of the unknown. The mysterious gates of Hell, made of bronze and iron,[27] were shattered.[28] Her bars smashed into the air. The figure of a radiant Jesus, surrounded by a huge angelic court, appeared in the

---

26   Ps 23:7–10.
27   *Desc. Chr. ad. Inf.* 5:3; *Gos. Bart.* 1:12.
28   Cf. Job 38:17; Ps 106:16.

presence of all the dead. Even those who were chained for lack of purification were suddenly set free.

Then Hell started to scream out: "We have been defeated! Who is this one so small in appearance, yet so great in power?" Jesus took Satan by his crown and handed him to the angels. He ordered them, saying: "Bind him hand and foot, with heavy iron chains." And turning to Hell, he ordered: "Let him be until my second coming. Only a small number of his agents shall be permitted to operate on the earth."[29]

Satan was imprisoned by 560 angels and tied with flaming iron chains. The devil looked like a dragon, some 1600 cubits long and 40 wide. He blew smoke out of his nostrils, and his mouth was like the recesses of a cliff.[30]

Jesus gathered all the dead and in a few words explained to them the redemptive plan—the Father's plan for the salvation of mankind, the course of humankind on earth, and the message of the kingdom of heaven, especially the resurrection of the dead.[31] Then he gave a special baptism for the remission of sins to those of the dead who believed and were in need of purification. After this ceremony, Jesus turned his gaze to hell in order to fulfill all that had been prescribed for Satan.

Hell, when he saw that all of his treasures had been stripped away—since not a single soul was left in his dungeon—turned his rage toward Satan, cursing and blasting him with insults for his schemes against Jesus, all of which had failed. And he put all the blame on Satan for this huge failure.

---

29   "We will not personally do anything. We have weaker ministers, which we command, and we will send them out to hunt and catch for us the souls of men, enticing them with different baits" (*Gos. Bart.* 4:44).

30   *Gos. Bart.* 4:12–13.

31   *Sib. Or.* I 378; *Didascalia* 26.

Jesus then formed a procession beginning with Adam followed by the patriarchs. The procession emerged from the depths of the earth and followed the invisible paths to paradise. There the righteous would wait for the final judgment. When they arrived at their heavenly destination, Jesus delivered this whole entourage over to the archangel Michael, who gave them accommodations in different places of paradise. The righteous will live in this wonderful place, happily awaiting the final glory after the Great Judgment. Other righteous people with a very special holiness who died prior to the Great Judgment will also find accommodation there, but most will have to wait in another place until the final judgment.[32]

Thus ended the story of the two brothers, Leucio and Carino, the sons of Simeon the Just. As one might expect, Annas, Caiaphas, and the other members of the Sanhedrin were dumbfounded. They remained silent for quite a while. Then, recovering from their astonishment, they believed very little of the story they had just heard. The two brothers were politely dismissed, and they got out of there immediately.

The priests and other members of the council were very agitated with the news that was coming to them. While all this was going on, Jesus resurrected some people in a most peculiar way. The Risen One appeared to Levi,[33] the son of Alpheus, who was fishing in the Sea of Galilee, and his brother James. James had made a vow during the Last Supper that he would not eat any food until he saw Jesus triumphant and resurrected from the dead. Well, one day James was at his home in Jerusalem, along with Peter and some of the other followers of the Nazarene. James was saddened by everything that happened to Jesus, but happy from what the women had reported about Jesus' appearances. Suddenly, Jesus appeared in their midst. The door never opened. He just

---

32   *Gos. Bart.* 1:31–34.

33   *Gos. Pet.* 60.

appeared. After greeting everyone in the room, Jesus said: "Touch me and see that I am not a ghost without body.[34] Set the table here and put out some bread."

They arranged a table and Jesus took some bread, blessed it, broke it, and gave it to James the Just, saying: "My brother, eat this bread, for the Son of Man has risen from the dead."[35] James' fast ended then and there. James and his companions took great comfort in the words of the Nazarene.

Jesus also appeared to all of the apostles on the Mount of Olives.[36] The disciples were very pleased because Jesus was revealing to them certain mysteries that most people did not know. Because they were privy to such information, they declared themselves happier than the rest of humanity. The Savior was alone, sitting a short distance away from the disciples. It was the fifteenth lunar day in January, when the Morning Star was at its peak. A great light shone forth from the Father of lights, and it engulfed Jesus from behind. It was so bright that the disciples could barely see. They could barely even make out the shape of Jesus, who was just a short distance away. All they saw was a silhouette of his body in contrast to the blinding rays of light behind him. There were multiple rays of light beaming forth, all of them different, and they went around the earth and extended up to the heavens. The light lifted Jesus up and took him away before his disciples' astonished eyes. It was around the third hour of the day. Three hours passed, and the disciples began to notice how the sky shook and all the heavenly powers trembled. Even the ground beneath their feet shook, so much so that the disciples of Jesus thought the end had finally arrived. Then, suddenly, it all stopped. The heavens and the earth ceased to quake. Then, high in the empyreal, a heavenly host erupted with songs and hymns of praise that came down to earth and reached the ears of the disciples. Although they could hear the singing, Peter and his companions were terribly frightened and

---

34   *(Cop.) Gos. Heb.* 19 (de Santos, 39).

35   *(Cop.) Gos. Heb.* 17 (de Santos, 38).

36   *Pistis Sophia* 61.

thought that God was about destroy everything. All of this lasted until the ninth hour of the following day.

The disciples dared not move from the Mount of Olives. They remained there the whole time, crying in terror. And when they least expected it, in the twinkling of an eye, the heavens opened and Jesus descended again before their eyes, surrounded by multicolored lights. The disciples were terrified, but Jesus told them: "Do not fear. Take comfort. I am." And the disciples said to him: "If it is you, please take away all this light. It is blinding us, and we cannot see anything." Jesus did as they asked, and immediately the disciples took courage. They worshiped him with fear and joy and said: "Master, where have you been, and why did you go there? Why have there been so many earthquakes and so much excitement?" Jesus answered them: "Rejoice, because I went for a moment to the place from where I come. But from now on, little by little, I will speak freely about the truth until you know it all. I am not going to speak with you in parables. I am going to speak directly to you with nothing to hide about the place from where I come. The ineffable and inexpressible One, the source of all mysteries, has given me this power to speak the truth from the beginning to the fullest, from the inside to the outside and from the outside to the inside."

The disciples were asking him all sorts of questions and Jesus just kept answering them. From here Jesus began instructing his disciples in private, giving them a new secret doctrine, a whole system of cosmological and soteriological theories. Most of these teachings are pure theological speculations concerning the substance and true nature of the Pleroma, or Fullness, the twenty emanations bearing different names that proceed from the Pleroma,[37] the mystery of the plan of salvation (i.e., salvation history), all the way to the powers of the air (i.e., fallen heavenly powers) and how the Savior outwitted them and overcame them[38] by his coming into the world. Similarly, these teachings treat

---

37   *Book of Jeu*, chps. 4ff.

38   *Soph. Jes. Chr.*, *Biblioteca de Nag Hammadi* III 4, 90,14–91,20.

matters like how humans can defend themselves against those celestial powers, seals and formulas they need in order to enter the Pleroma after death.[39] Others discuss how Jesus will appear when he returns,[40] what heaven will be like,[41] and what will take place immediately before the end of the world.[42] And there are others

---

39 *Book of Jeu*, chps. 4ff.

40 "Then we said to him: 'Lord, great is what you have revealed to us. Will you describe for us what power and appearance you will have when you return?' He answered and said to us: 'I will come like the sun when it rises, and my brightness will be seven times its brightness. I will come riding on the clouds, and my cross will go before me, setting down on the earth ahead of me'" (*Ep. Apost.* 16).

41 "The disciples said: 'You have been our salvation and life. What is this hope (for the future) that you are telling us about now?' And he answered us: 'Have hope, and be encouraged. Truly I say to you that I will bring you to a place of rest, where there is no need to eat or drink, where there is no shame or songs of sadness, where there is no need for clothing, where there is no corruption'" (*Ep. Apost.* 19).

42 "Again we said to him: 'Lord, what you are telling us is so important. And you are proclaiming and explaining such wonderful things to us in such a way that it has calmed our fears and shown us your grace. After your resurrection you have revealed to us everything so that we might be saved. And you have told us about the signs and wonders that will take place before the end of the world, things that will take place both in heaven and on earth. Teach us now so we can understand it.' And the Lord said: 'I will teach you not just what will happen to you, but also to those who you will teach and who will believe . . . . In those years and days both the believers and the unbelievers will see a great horn in the sky and the face of the great stars, which will be visible even during daylight. All will see a great dragon, whose body will stretch from the earth to the heavens. Stars like great balls of fire will fall from the sky, and gigantic burning hail will come crashing to the earth. The Sun and the Moon will fight among themselves, their blows producing lightning, thunder, and earthquakes. The cities will collapse, causing the death of many people. In the rest of the world there will be a huge drought. Not even the slightest drop of rain will fall from the sky, and many will die, so many they cannot even be buried'" (*Ep. Apost.* 34).

that are like magical formulas and invocations that can be used to get the divinity to do things.[43]

Twelve years passed, and it was time for Jesus to finally leave this world. During this time he had given his disciples many powers. Into their hands was placed the key to the kingdom of heaven.[44] They were given permission to decide who would enter the light and who would be banished to the darkness, since they possessed the key to the forgiveness of sins,[45] as well as the mysteries of the resurrection of the dead and the power of healing.[46] But before he left, while they were in Galilee,[47] Jesus said to them: "The one who sent me is coming in three days and three hours to take me with him."

And as soon as he stopped talking a heavy storm exploded in the sky. There was thunder and lightning everywhere. Lighting lit up the sky, and the earth began to shake again, creating a huge

---

43   "When Jesus was with his disciples on the shores of the sea, he offered the following prayer: 'Hear me, Father—Father of all—You, infinite Light, aeēiouō iaō aōi ōia psinōther thernōps nōpsither zagourē pagourē nethmomaōth nepsiomaōth marachachtha thōbarrabau tharnachachan zorokothora ieou sabaōth.'

While Jesus was praying this prayer, Thomas, Andrew, James, and Simon the Zealot were in the west with their faces toward the east, and Philip and Bartholomew were in the south facing north, and the rest of the disciples, including the female disciples, stood behind Jesus. But Jesus was by the altar.
Then Jesus shouted out to the four corners of the earth, along with his disciples, who were dressed in robes: 'Iaō iaō iaō,' which translated means, 'Iota, because you proceed from the All; Alfa, because to him you will return; Omega, because you will have a place in the consummation of consummation.'

When he finished those words, Jesus continued, saying: 'Iaphtha iaphtha mounaēr mounaēr ermanouēr ermanouēr,' which means, 'You, Father of all, listen to me for the sake of my disciples, who I have brought before you, so that they might believe in every word of your truth, and so that they might have everything for which I am praying now, because I know your name, the name of the Father of the luminous treasure'" (*Pistis Sophia* 136).

44   *Pistis Sophia* 141.
45   *Pistis Sophia* 37 and 141.
46   *Pistis Sophia* 110.
47   This is a tradition recognized by Tertullian (*Apology* 21).

chasm in the ground. A thin cloud descended to the ground with a huge light that surrounded Jesus. And the cloud took him. He disappeared out of sight. They could see a luminous cross following behind their Master as he was taken up to heaven.[48] Then they heard the voices of many angels as they rejoiced, praising the Ineffable One. And when it seemed like Jesus was just about out of sight, a voice was heard from above saying: "Go in peace." And so Jesus' earthly life came to its end.[49]

---

48   *Acta Pionii* 13; cf. *Sib. Or.* 26–28.
49   *Ep. Apost.* 51; *Pistis Sophia* 2–6.

The End of Antipas and Pilate

We are approaching the end of our story. It all comes full circle with the mother of Jesus, to whom a whole chapter is devoted detailing the events surrounding her death and assumption, some of which are juicy and important. But first, what happened to Herod Antipas and Pilate? They played such an influential role in the last moments of Jesus' earthly life. Before we turn the attention to Mary, a brief account of the last days of these influential figures is in order. The records provide some information that might be of interest to the reader.

Herod Antipas wrote a letter to Pilate that details the tragedy that befell him and his family for having his people execute the innocent Galilean teacher. A few days after the events of Golgotha, Herodias, the Tetrarch's beloved daughter, was playing on the banks of the Jordan. Suddenly, the river flooded and the water rose up to the girl's neck. Her mother, who was there along with some maids, grabbed her by the head so she would not be swept away by the current. It was no hope, though. The girl's head detached from her body. All her mother could do was hold on to the head, but the rest of Herodias's body was swept away by the raging waters. Herod's wife burst into tears and fell to her knees, holding her daughter's head and writhing in grief.

Not long after that, Lebonax, the Tetrarch's son, became bedridden, having fallen ill to some mysterious and incurable disease. He languished in bed, longing to be healed but no cure was in sight. The monarch had suffered from dropsy for a long time. His dropsy went from worse to dire, so bad that worms began to come out of his mouth. And to make matters worse, the queen lost her left eye in some stupid domestic accident. Because she was crying so much, her wound became infected. Within a few days she had completely lost the capacity to see out of that eye.

It was not long before all of the members of Herod's family died. Pilate buried them, just as Herod had requested. Herod also sent Pilate a parting gift—the most precious earrings that belonged to his daughter and the king's own ring.[1] And that is how the lives of Herod and his family came to their end, which served the king well given what he had done to Jesus and his lack of repentance thereafter.

And of Pilate the following is said to have happened.[2] Tiberius Caesar became very sick and sent messengers throughout the whole Empire in search of a cure. A Jewish man who wandered into the emperor's court was telling people about a certain magician named Jesus who had healed many people in Palestine by the laying on of hands. He thought this man might be able to heal the emperor. The emperor was definitely willing to try anything. When Tiberius heard the news about Jesus, he commissioned a highly trusted man named Volusianus to find this man and bring him to Rome. Volusianus traveled to Caesarea on the Empire's best ship, taking only eight days to reach the Phoenician coast because the winds were so favorable. He was told to find Jesus and persuade him at whatever cost necessary to come to Rome.

Volusianus was quick to do what the emperor had commanded him. When he landed, he heard that Pilate was in Jerusalem. So, he jumped in a chariot and off he went, racing to the capital. He found Pilate and told him about the emperor's request. Pilate began to tremble and was terribly afraid, but he began to tell the messenger the truth about what happened. "That man was actually a criminal," he told Volusianus. "He was leading the people astray, proclaiming to be a king himself and refusing to pay taxes to

1   *Letter of Herod to Pilate* (de Santos, 481ff.).
2   *Paradosis of Pilate* and *Death of Pilate* (de Santos, 484ff.).

Caesar,[3] which was a threat to us. Therefore, after conferring with the elders of the city, I gave the order for him to be crucified."

Volusianus could not believe it. He knew what the emperor expected of him, and now fulfilling his mission would be impossible, since Jesus was dead. He was trying to figure out what to do. One possibility was to have Pilate arrested and to bring him back to Rome for causing all this mess. A Jewish man was there and informed him of a certain woman named Veronica. This woman had a miraculous portrait of Jesus. The idea was he could buy it and take it back to Rome, and perhaps the emperor would be healed just from setting his eyes on it. This idea seemed better than arresting Pilate and taking him to Rome, which had no possibility of healing Tiberius. Volusianus sent some people to find Veronica. Locating her was not all that difficult. Once they found her, they brought her to Volusianus. She told the emperor's messenger: "I actually have two portraits of my teacher. A friend of mine painted one on canvas. I felt bad when my teacher would leave to go preach, because I could not see him. For that reason, I asked my friend to paint me a portrait of Jesus so that I could have him with me always. And I also have a picture of just his face, painted on a cloth that I gave Jesus to wipe the sweat from his brow and clean some of the blood off of his face as he walked to the cross."

Volusianus asked with great impatience: "How much do you want for either of these portraits? I will pay you whatever you want." "These images cannot be bought with gold or silver," said Veronica, "only with a heart of worship. I will not sell them, but I will accompany you to Rome and take one of the portraits to see Caesar and heal him of his illness."

Volusianus was pleased with her offer and postponed issuing the warrant for Pilate's arrest. The messenger and Veronica set out to Rome, bringing along one of the portraits of Jesus. The emperor greeted them immediately when they arrived. He was happy to see his messenger because his sickness had not let up one inch.

---

3   Luke 23:2.

Volusianus gave his report to Tiberius: "That Jewish doctor named Jesus, whom you sent me to find and bring back, was handed over to his countrymen by your governor Pilate, and they crucified him. But do not worry. I brought with me a certain woman who has a portrait of Jesus. If you look upon it with faith, you will be healed of your illness."

Caesar was not completely convinced, but he immediately ordered them to roll out the silk carpet so that Veronica could enter with the portrait of Jesus. Tiberius looked at the portrait of Jesus, and immediately he was healed. But Pilate did not escape being punished. He was sent for not long after and, by imperial order, was placed under arrest and brought to Rome. Caesar ordered that Pilate appear straightaway at the palace. Pilate was well aware of what awaited him in Rome. For this reason, he had acquired the seamless garment of the Nazarene, the one for which the soldiers had cast lots at the cross.[4] He brought it along with him as a sort of charm, hoping it would protect him from any danger he might face in Rome.

When he appeared before the emperor, wearing the seamless robe of Jesus underneath his clothing, Tiberias's anger mysteriously dissipated. He asked Pilate: "How dare you commit so heinous a crime as ordering the execution of an innocent man?" Troubled, Pilate answered him: "O emperor! I am not guilty of this. It was that terrible mob of Jews that caused all this." "And why did you go along with their plan?" argued Tiberius. "Their nation is rude and rebellious," replied Pilate. "And they act like they are not subject to your rule. I thought it was best to remain calm, until they said this Jesus was the Christ, some sort of anointed person or king. You know what something like that would mean for your throne."

Right when the word "Christ" was uttered in the presence of Tiberius, some of the images of the different gods that were placed in the courtroom of the emperor fell to the ground and shattered, causing a dust storm where Caesar sat surrounded by his senators. Everyone present was very frightened and Tiberius adjourned the

---

4   John 19:23.

meeting, giving special orders that Pilate be closely monitored. That night Tiberius had a dream whereby it was revealed to him that Pilate was protected with the robe of Jesus, and that he could not be punished so long as he wore it. So, he ordered that they strip it off Pilate by force and for him to appear before the court the next day dressed only in his own clothes.

The next day the trial resumed against the former governor of Judea. When Pilate saw Tiberius he was enraged and asked no further questions. After a short deliberation, he issued the following statement: "Pilate is guilty and deserves to die. Give him the most shameful of deaths."

It was decided that Pilate would be impaled, a death reserved for slaves in the Empire. He was to be executed immediately, but the night before a friend of Pilate's family managed to give him a sharp knife. Pilate killed himself with that knife, opening up his guts with a single cut. When Tiberius heard the news, he said: "Truly he has died with great shame, for his own hand has not forgiven the disgrace he previously committed."

Some soldiers removed the body of Pilate. They put him in a sack, tied a huge stone to it, and threw his body into the Tiber, in an area renowned for its depth and enormous churning waters. It is said that certain unclean and evil spirits moved through the waters, causing storms, winds, lightning, thunder, and hail, so bad that the locals were greatly afraid of the site. They decided to dredge the river with hooks and recover the body. And so they did. Placing it in a new sackcloth, the body was transported by wagon far, far away. They threw the body of Pilate deep into some dry and bare mountains. It is said that the place is filled with all sorts of devils.[5]

---

5   *Paradosis of Pilate* 1–8 and *Death of Pilate* (de Santos, 490–494).

10

The Final Days of Mary's Sojourn

Mary lived a number of years after the crucifixion of Jesus. She lived the remainder of her days in Jerusalem and its environs, usually under the roof of the beloved disciple[1] (though she had another house in Bethlehem). She would visit the empty tomb of her son every single day. She burned incense and spent time in prayer and meditation. As she grew older, even though she was healthy and suffered from no illnesses, she would beg her son take her to be with him.[2]

Mary visited the tomb where Jesus had been laid so often that it bothered many of the Jews. They wanted to make sure that it did not turn into some sort of destination for religious pilgrimages among his followers. So, one day they put guards around the tomb to keep his followers away. Such a move did nothing to keep Mary away. She became invisible to the guards, though she did not know it, and was able to pass undisturbed. One Friday the Virgin was at the grave of her son as usual. And while she was praying, the archangel Gabriel appeared.[3] He greeted her, saying, "Hail Mary," and announced that her wishes would finally be fulfilled. She was informed that her departure was near. In fact, it would take place within three days.

And with this announcement he handed to her a palm leaf, saying: "Take this palm leaf that was given to me by the one who

---

1   Cf. John 19:27.
2   *Book of Saint John the Evangelist* 1–2.
3   According to the Ethiopian Book of Rest (3), this angel is Jesus.

planted Paradise, and give it to the apostles of Jesus who will accompany you to the place of your rest. Thanks to them, many will be healed of their ailments."[4] Mary asked the angel: "What shall I do to escape the evil powers that are now seeking after my soul?" "Do not worry," the angel replied. "When the time comes, you will be surrounded by the apostles and I too will come for your soul—and not just me, but all the angelic hosts—and they will go before you singing hymns."

With that Mary's nerves were calmed, and she went to her home carrying the palm leaf the angel had given her. As she passed through the Mount of Olives,[5] the ground shook and quaked, as if it was longing for Mary's assumption. All of the trees and plants worshipped the plant from Paradise. When she arrived home, she ordered one of the handmaidens, whose name was Zipporah,[6] to visit the family of Mary and ask them to visit her. The girl did as she was asked, and within hours all of Mary's acquaintances and relatives gathered in the house. She told them: "Take this palm leaf. Keep watch and stay with me for three days without falter, for my soul must fight off the evil spirits that will attempt to seize it. Your presence will help me in this struggle. We are going to move to my house in Bethlehem,[7] because I want to depart this world from the place of my son's birth." Everyone began to weep at the thought of the mother of Jesus leaving, but Mary comforted them, saying: "Do not weep. Recite the psalms in place of your mourning, because my going away will become a blessing to you."

And with those words Mary reclined in her bed, and everyone remained around her bedside. It was about the third hour and all of creation began to moan. The day turned dark outside, and heavy rains fell on Bethlehem with lightning flashing across the sky and thunder shaking the earth below.[8]

---

4   *Book of John, Archbishop of Thessalonica* 3.
5   *Book of John, Archbishop of Thessalonica* 3.
6   Transit A, *Narrative of Pseudo-Joseph of Arimathea* 5.
7   *Book of Saint John the Evangelist* 26.
8   Transit A, *Narrative of Pseudo-Joseph of Arimathea* 6.

Before long, just as the angel had foretold, the apostles began to arrive from all corners of the earth. Wherever they were, the Spirit snatched them up and transported them by air to Mary's home in Bethlehem. John came from Ephesus, Peter from Rome, Andrew from Achaia, Paul from Corinth, etc.[9] They all came from wherever they were, including Thomas, who was transported on a glorious cloud from the very center of India where he had preached in the kingdom of Gundafor.[10] Each of them was telling Mary about what they had been doing in the places where they preached the gospel, and how the Spirit had let them know that she was nearing the end of her stay in this world and that they needed to be by her side during this time. Mary rejoiced and wept at the same time, seeing all the apostles together with her.

When all of them had gathered together with Mary, she urged them to begin praying. And so they did. The whole night was spent at her bedside. The apostles begged Peter, the first among the apostles, to deliver an uplifting sermon to them. The prince of the apostles agreed to do so, and the message lasted all night. In it, recalling his memories of Jesus, he explained to everyone the meaning of Jesus' parables and the mystery of the kingdom of heaven.[11] Peter's discourse lasted from Friday night to Saturday, and all the Jews rested as prescribed by the Law. The apostles prayed, and while they put incense into a censer, there was another terrible celestial phenomenon. The sky cleared, and there was a terrible thunder and a great voice seemed to echo across the whole earth. Then a whole host of angels appeared. Some seraphim surrounded the house. They were even noticed by some passersby. Some of them took off for Jerusalem to inform the priests of the wonders that were taking place in the city of David.

When Sunday arrived, at the third hour, Jesus himself appeared at his mother's home in Bethlehem, so that he could

---

9   *Book of Saint John the Evangelist* 14–22; *Book of John, Archbishop of Thessalonica* 7.

10   Cf. *Acts Thom.* 17ff.

11   *(Eth.) B. Rest* 54–65.

oversee his mother's passage to the life to come. Many other angels accompanied him, and they sang a song: "Like a lily among the thorns, so is my love among the daughters of men."[12] Then a great light shone down on the house, so bright it was like the radiance of the sun and the moon combined fell upon the house.[13] A soft but very strong perfume filled the room, and everyone fell on their faces. For an hour and a half no one was able get up.[14]

As the light faded, the assumption of Mary's soul into heaven began. Mary smiled as Jesus fulfilled his final mission, and then he took her soul and placed it in Michael's hands, but not before having it wrapped in a special type of veils, whose radiance was impossible to describe. The apostles could see that the soul of the Virgin had all the parts of a physical body, minus those that distinguished sex. It had the likeness of a human body, but with a brightness that surpassed seven times that of the sun.[15]

The death of the mother of Jesus was a natural process. It slowly extinguished like a dimly burning wick. The angels sang hymns and psalms; a cloud began to rise from Mary's room; and the earth shook ever so slightly. It was learned later on that a number of the lame, the deaf, and paralytics were healed of their diseases at this very moment. The blind could see, the lepers were made clean, and those possessed by evil spirits were set free from their bondage.[16] A few Christian virgins, along with three of Mary's handmaidens, were responsible for preparing Mary's body for burial.[17]

Some of the Jewish priests and many people from Jerusalem heard that a large number of Christians had assembled in Bethlehem and that all the Christian leaders were there as well. It seemed like the opportune time to put an end to these heretics. Satan entered

---

12   Song of Songs 2:2 = Transit A, *Narrative of Pseudo-Joseph of Arimathea* 11.
13   *Book of Saint John the Evangelist* 26.
14   Transit A, *Narrative of Pseudo-Joseph of Arimathea* 11.
15   *Book of John, Archbishop of Thessalonica* 12.
16   *Book of Saint John the Evangelist* 27.
17   *(Eth.) B. Rest* 71.

them and filled them with an extremely violent rage. They handed out weapons and decided to set fire to the houses where the people were assembled and put the apostles to death. They were jealous for the Law and thought the chief disciples of Jesus, along with his mother, were causing the collapse of Israel and trying to insert new fables into the very heart of a well-established religion.[18] A heavily armed squadron of Jews set out for Bethlehem. When they were about a mile away from the gate of the city they saw something dreadful that made them freeze right in their steps. There, emerging from a cloud, came a group of angels armed with fiery swords, who took their stand in attack positions. The Jewish squadron was gripped with fear. Nearly blinded by the light, they retraced their steps and went back to Jerusalem. They could not see well though. Instead of making a clean getaway, they just ended up running into the sides of neighboring houses and crashing into one another. And so, amid great confusion, they finally managed to return to the capital, and they told their leaders everything that happened.

Meanwhile, the apostles and everyone else that had been present for Mary's departure to the other world made arrangements to transport her body. A new tomb had been purchased in a garden that was near the road that connected Bethlehem to Jerusalem. The garden was very near the capital, practically next to the city wall. They placed her body in a coffin and the procession set out. With psalms and prayers, the procession slowly made its way toward the tomb, while the inhabitants of Bethlehem maintained a respectful distance and silence. But a priest named Reuben was indignant and tried to knock over the coffin. But right when he went to do so, his arms dried up and turned like stone from his hands all the way to his elbows. And he began to cry and weep when he saw what had happened to his arms. He started walking alongside the procession, begging the apostles to have mercy on him.[19] Peter looked at him with compassion, and with only a

---

18   Transit A, *Narrative of Pseudo-Joseph of Arimathea* 13.
19   Transit A, *Narrative of Pseudo-Joseph of Arimathea* 14–15.

slight movement of his head, the arms of the priest returned to their natural state. The priest knelt and kissed the feet of Peter, requesting to be baptized immediately in the name of Jesus.

Meanwhile, the Jews had embarked on a new mission against the apostles and the funeral procession, but this time the group of Jerusalemites was accompanied by a Roman commander and a few of his soldiers. The new governor was hesitant to grant permission for this detachment of Jews to accompany them, not wanting to get involved in anything concerning Jesus and his disciples. Nevertheless, the Jews convinced him that the presence of imperial soldiers would help maintain a certain degree of order in the land as they punished the Christians. So, with that they went out again to exterminate the Christians who had come together to be with Mary in her last moments.

The road to Jerusalem was long for those that were accompanying the body of Mary, and they were afraid that there might be other attacks by anti-Christian zealots. And, of course, they were right in their suspicion. Another mission was already underway. So, the Spirit gathered up all of the apostles and their companions and transported them instantly in a cloud to Mary's home in Jerusalem. The commander and his men arrived in Bethlehem and found nothing—no Christians and not even a hint of the funeral procession. The Roman commander, feeling like a fool, turned his fury on the Jewish leaders and had his soldiers hit them with sticks and disperse the mob. Then he returned to Jerusalem with his soldiers and reported to the governor that it was all a hoax.[20]

The ceremony for Mary lasted several days in Jerusalem and consisted of hymns, fasting, and prayer. Her house in the holy city was overflowing with Christians who came to pay their respect. During those five days, people were moving in and out of the house. For many Jews this was unbearable, becoming even more enraged. They decided to burn the house to the ground, resolved to cremate not just the body of Mary, but that of every single

---

20   *Book of Saint John the Evangelist* 33.

person inside the home. The governor caught wind of their plan, but he did not act because of the uproar and rage of the mob. He just watched from afar as their plan unfolded. When everything was just about ready, a large flame of fire suddenly shot out of the house—the work of an angel—and it consumed some in the mob that was planning to assault the Christians gathered at Mary's home. Faced with such a wonder, there was a split among the attackers. Many were convinced that the hand of God was with the Christians and that they should give serious consideration to this new faith. Then they dispersed, carrying the remains of those who had perished by the divine fire.[21]

When Sunday arrived, the apostles carefully moved Mary's body to a new tomb in the garden next to the city wall, in the valley of Jehoshaphat. The next day, early in the morning, Thomas went to the grave with the intention of making his morning prayers. But to his surprise he found that the stone that closed up the entrance of the tomb had been rolled back. He went inside the tomb, curious and fearful at the same time, and found that the tomb was empty. There was no sign of Mary's body or the coffin. Then he set out to tell his fellow apostles the news he had discovered. While he was on his way, he had a vision. He saw the body of Mary as it was taken out of the tomb and then carried to Paradise in the midst of angelic choirs. The mother of Jesus spoke to him and said: "Tell your brothers what has happened. And as a token from me, I leave you this relic of mine."

And with these words she handed Thomas the cord that the apostles had used to wrap her body. And then she suddenly disappeared out of sight as fast as she had appeared. A very soft perfume filled the path leading up to the garden, and Thomas found the cord in his hands, as it was in his vision. He rejoiced because the body of the mother of Jesus would not suffer decay and would wait in Paradise for the final resurrection. Thomas went to the house where the other apostles were and told them about his vision. Some found it hard to believe, but when he showed

---

21 *Book of Saint John the Evangelist* 37.

them the cord, there was no doubt. Most of them still decided to go to the empty tomb and see it for themselves. And seeing the empty tomb, they were all convinced beyond the shadow of a doubt that the assumption of the body and soul of the mother of Jesus to heaven had taken place, news that has been passed down from generation to generation, all the way to the present day.

CONCLUSION

Apart from the secret teachings of this other Jesus found in the apocryphal Gospels, the story of this unknown life of Jesus ends with the same character, Mary, the mother of the Nazarene. I think, however, that some of the anecdotes, miracles of Jesus, and other stories that are transcribed in the preceding pages will undoubtedly be known to the readers (perhaps more than in earlier years?) or at the least they will have some idea of them in their back of their minds. This is an indication of the significance and importance the apocryphal Gospels have had throughout the history of the first centuries of the Church, and how this tradition has been repeated over the centuries up to the present day. The liturgy, beliefs about St. Joseph and the Virgin Mary, the popularized theology of various segments within the Church, the development of dogma—all of these fields are reflected in the traditions that contain the accounts of the apocryphal Gospels. Therefore, some final thoughts on this material would not look out of place in this book and will also serve to corroborate some points brought out in the Foreword.

The desires of everyday people played a huge part in the birth of the apocryphal Gospel literature—and the apocryphal books of the Bible in general. In most cases, when the canonical Gospels that are called "Synoptic" (Matthew, Mark, Luke) had been established, people realized that these letters contained very little information about Jesus in areas that were of interest to them.

Above all, they were interested in the early years of Jesus' life, and this hidden life had barely received attention from Matthew and Luke. John and Mark ignored this part of his life altogether! Thus began the desire to fill in this gap, and others like it, and the authors of the apocryphal literature were helped by a certain literary tradition. The habit of imitating the biblical books, in Jewish circles, dates back to well before New Testament times. The rich Judeo-Hellenistic religious literature (c. third century B.C. to A.D. first century), known as the Old Testament Apocrypha, is one example. Examples from within this corpus include the Book of Jubilees, which rewrites Genesis, or 3 or 4 Ezra, which expands the story of this learned and famous scribes' life.

And so Christians, like the Jews in this regard, did not have many problems with filling in the gaps of their own official Gospels. One phrase from the Gospel of John offered, albeit indirectly, a rationale for why these apocryphal Gospels came into existence: "And there are also many other things which Jesus did, which if they were written in detail, I suppose that even the world itself would not contain the books that would be written" (John 21:25).

Of course, one reason for the composition of these texts was to help some marginalized Christian groups ("heretics") embody their beliefs. In order to defend their ideas, they made up "Gospels" that presented Jesus in a way that aligned with their interpretation of him and his teachings. So, they promoted their religious ideas through these "apocryphal" books (i.e., the hidden and esoteric revelations and perspectives on Jesus).

Similarly, others wanted to oppose the ideas of those same groups, which gradually came to be regarded as heretical by the main group of believers. Therefore, they composed "counter-Gospels" to defend orthodox ideas. A saying of Jesus, a scene from his life, a secret revelation that is made public at the appropriate time might just pump the brakes on the proliferation of ideas perceived as unorthodox.

Last but not least, with regard to a few apocryphal Gospels, given the early date of their composition—some dating around the middle of the second century—some of them could very well be the collections of oral traditions about Jesus that were not fortunate enough to be recognized and generally accepted by common believers, who had accepted the Synoptics and the Gospel of John. But the number of these types of Gospels is very, very few.

Unfortunately for these writings, most Christians believe that almost all of them were written too late—toward the end of the second century through the fourth century—at a time when the guidelines regulating the inclusion of texts in the list of sacred Christian writings was already well-defined. Their claim of canonicity, that is, to be considered sacred, was frustrated because they could not offer any proof that they were written by or during the time of the first apostles. By A.D. 180-200, most churches had already decided what they viewed as "canonical." By A.D. 200, the New Testament was basically formed, though with some hesitation surrounding Hebrews, Revelation, 2 Peter, Jude, James, and 2 and 3 John. Likewise, it had already been decided which writings could be rejected as "false" or "spurious."[1] Though it should be mentioned that some of those texts continued to circulate for centuries.

But just because these texts are not "accepted" by the Church, or considered "sacred," does not mean they are unimportant given their antiquity. For the history of theology, culture, and religious movements, these texts are invaluable because they give us knowledge about the popular trends within the Church; they provide information on the development of theology in areas that were not rigidly controlled by the official hierarchy; and they uncover the natural spiritual concerns of Christian people. The history of the Church, liturgy, and religious ideas in general has a lot to learn from these apocryphal "records" as representatives of very different traditions, some of which have been kept alive to this very day. And if that were not enough, the Apocrypha are

---

1   Cf. A. Piñero, "Cómo y por qué se formó el Nuevo Testamento," 339-400.

often the only witness of a popular faith that has been converted into dogma with the passing of time.

The way this literature has been preserved has varied as well. It is not always preserved to the present day through direct transmission. Generally speaking, apocryphal texts had a much harder time in the West than in the East. When most of them had been translated into Latin, they finally spread to all the Christian nations of Europe. When that happened, the apocryphal Gospels had a huge influence on literature, and later (especially in the Middle Ages) on art and iconography. By that time, however, the original text of many of them had already been lost. They were circulating, at that point, in edited and manipulated forms. The hagiographic literature of the Middle Ages mostly drew from the apocryphal text. In the Byzantine area, the menologies and lives of the saints with hints of these texts enjoyed great success. In the Latin tradition, they preserved some of the apocryphal texts directly, such as the Gospel of James and the Assumption of Mary, but especially small stories or legends about Jesus that circulated through the works of Vincent de Beauvais's *Speculum Historiale* and James of Voragine's *Legenda aurea*. In various localized churches (e.g., the Irish, Coptic, Syrian, Armenian, Georgian and Ethiopian), these apocryphal texts continued to live on in countless translations. Research in the present day continues to find and evaluate multiple manuscripts, unveiling these traditions that were nearly lost after the Reformation and the Council of Trent.[2]

The apocryphal Gospels played a significant role in the evolution and strengthening of dogma, as L. Moraldi[3] and A.

---

2   Cf. the section "Weiterleben und Wirkung der neutestamentlichen Apokryphen" ("Pervivencia e influjo posterior de los apócrifos neotestamentarios" in W. Schneemelcher, *Neutestamentliche Apokryphen*, I 52ff.). It should be noted that the apocryphal tradition in Spain must have flourished and spread to Ireland. While the remains of it are barely noticeable in the Iberian Peninsula, the Irish church has retained remarkable examples: cf. the work of M. McNamara, *The Apocrypha in the Irish Church* (Dublin 1975).

3   Moraldi, *Apocrifi*, 26-27.

de Santos[4] point out, for example, with the virginity of Mary (Nativity Gospels), Christ's descent into hell after his death to rescue the souls of the deceased patriarchs and the just who died prior to his coming (Gospel of Nicodemus), the Assumption of the Virgin (Gospel of John the Theologian; Gospel of Joseph of Arimathea),

> the names that we give to parents of the Virgin, Joachim and Anne . . . the feast of the *Presentation* of the young Virgin . . . the birth of Jesus in a cave that never lacked an *ox* or *donkey*; the flight into Egypt with the idols that were struck down; the three Magi Kings, with their names Melchor, Gaspar and Baltasar; the story of the thieves Dimas and Gestas (who were crucified next to Jesus); the name of the soldier, called Longinus, who pierced the side of Jesus; the story of Veronica . . . These and other details rest on nothing but the historical foundation of the accounts of the apocryphal Gospels.[5]

Since the Middle Ages, many of these stories have made their way into religious booklets and pulpits, almost to the present day. This latter phenomenon explains how many of these stories sound so familiar to people that have never read the apocryphal Gospels. Today, when there is a new type of preaching and spiritual reading, is precisely the moment in which this ancient tradition starts to get lost among the people, a tradition collected systematically since time immortal.

These are ancient manuscripts, some of them written some 1800 years ago. These manuscripts have served as the primary sources for the second part of this book, as we stitched their ideas together in a way that retains the plot but exposes the reader to the overall material. We have tried to be faithful to the whole apocryphal corpus, without adding or taking away, only whatever

4   *Evangelios apócrifos*, 8-9.
5   This is translated from de Santos, *Evangelios apócrifos*, 9 (emphasis original).

was necessary in order to make the text readable, now eighteen centuries later. And unless the dry sands of Egypt or some Middle Eastern desert provides us with new discoveries of papyri or manuscripts, then what we have in this book is the substance of all we now have in painting the picture of the hidden life of the "other" Jesus.

I also wish to stress once again that the historicity of the documents used for this book is a whole different matter. This writer believes, with the vast majority of scholars, that they are not historical documents. They are popular legends, sometimes anonymous and commonly forged; sometimes they were knowingly composed as legends. The main reason for not viewing them as historical is their late dates of composition. It had been many years since Jesus' death, and there was no reliable evidence around for the composition of texts on his hidden life. Another reason is that they did not begin to gather information about Jesus until after his death, and by that time he was viewed as a transcendental figure, related to the divinity in some way, for the history of the salvation of mankind. By that time there was no faithful record dealing with the years of Jesus' childhood—without practical significance for believers—or other moments of his hidden life, since they had no relevance to his preaching. Therefore, the vast majority of what was written about his hidden life was due to fantasy and legend, written down in these texts that we now call the "apocryphal Gospels."

The great battle for the image of a "canonical" Jesus took place between different groups of Christians from the moment these other texts started to be composed—around the second century. They competed with those Gospels that had acquired the status of canonical or sacred, namely Mark, Matthew, Luke, and, later on, John. For the Orthodox, from that point on to the sixth and eighth centuries, there was a fight to the death to rid the world, and especially the churches, of these apocryphal Gospels. Sometimes they edited them, trying to replace their content with Orthodox theology.

But this process ended many centuries ago, and except for pockets of heterodoxy—due mainly to quotations in the Church Fathers and the discovery of new manuscripts at Nag Hammadi in the twentieth century—what now remains of these forged documents in various ancient languages has been filtered through hundreds of years of orthodoxy.

Today we are witnessing a resurgence of interest in the New Testament Apocrypha, especially the Gospels. Much of this is due, in esoteric or related circles today, to the morbid desire to find in this body of writings, which are not accepted as sacred by the official Church, some truths, more or less interesting or compromised, that this same Church would have tried to hide from the faithful. And others think they can find in the secret teachings of Jesus, preserved in some of the apocryphal texts— such as those of Nag Hammadi—the hidden face of Christ.

Against this pursuit, we must insist on several things. First, these apocryphal texts cannot be hidden today. They are manuscripts preserved in museums and public institutions. They are no longer owned by Christian churches, but by science of Antiquity—philology and ancient history, to be specific—who should study them, as they do with any other document from past centuries in the West. Second, just as the Church fought and won the battle against them (starting in the fourth century), today they have no interest in keeping them hidden. In fact, the vast majority of modern editions of the apocryphal Gospels has been made by priests with the blessing of their respective bishops. Third, it is important to note the date of composition of the apocryphal Gospels. As we have argued, the vast majority were written very late. The oldest of them, such as the gnostic *Gospel of Thomas* and the *Protoevangelium of James*, in their present form were at least written after those Gospels that have been accepted as canonical. As it happens, the writings of Mark, Matthew, Luke, and John are still the oldest Gospels to date. The apocryphal Gospels should be placed in the category of fiction, although some scholars might argue that they transmit remnants of earlier material. But what can we say about their overall value and significance? They contain pictures of the history of theology and religious ideas from the second century or onward, but they do not reveal the "secrets" of the life of Jesus nor the origins of Christianity.

And one final thought. Basically, the entirety of this book is made up of fiction. It does not apply at all to the Jesus of history, but to a Jesus of legend, one that is sometimes unpleasant. And if the image of Jesus that these apocryphal Gospels puts forth is what we have tried to present our readers, we can ask as we indicated in the Foreword: Is the picture given by the apocryphal Gospels—very different indeed to the one that is commonly known—really more interesting and complex than the one that we get from a critical reading of the Gospels that are recognized as canonical? Would it be productive today to try and hide the apocryphal documents from the eyes of Christians? The readers can decide for themselves.

So, this writer leaves the last word to the reader. We have been tasked with reconstructing the history of a confusing, disjointed, repetitive, and sometimes not so interesting corpus of apocryphal Gospels. It is very likely though that the reader will arrive at the conclusion that the best way to study the historical Jesus, the only one that matters, must be through studying those documents written nearest to the time when he lived, that is, the canonical Gospels. But such a study must be done using philological and historical criticism.

Antonio Piñero

BIBLIOGRAPHY

Aguirre, R., C. Bernabé, and C. Gil. *Qué se sabe de Jesús de Nazaret.* Estella, Spain: Verbo Divino, 2009.

Bauer, Walter. *Das Leben Jesu im Zeitalter der neutestamentlichen Apokryphen.* Tübingen: Paul Siebeck, 1909, reprod. Wissenschaftliche Buchgesellschaft 1967.

Berendts, Alexander (ed.). *Die Zeugnisse vom Christentum im slavischen ‚De bello iudaico' des Josephus,* Texte und Untersuchungen (Leipzig) XXIX (new series XIV), 1906.

Bezold, Carl. *Die Schatzhöhle aus dem syrischen Texte dreier unedirten Handschriften ins Deutsche übersetzt und mit Anmerkungen versehen.* Vol. 1. Leipzig: J.C. Hinrichs, 1883.

Borg, Marcus J. and John Dominic Crossan. *The First Christmas: What the Gospels Really Teach About Jesus' Birth.* New York: HarperCollins, 2007.

Bovon, François, *Luke 1: A Commentary on the Gospel of Luke 1:1–9:50.* Hermeneia. Translated by Christine M. Thomas. Edited by Helmut Koester. Minneapolis, MN: Fortress, 2002.

Brown, Raymond E. *The Birth of the Messiah: A Commentary on the Infancy Narratives in the Gospels of Matthew and Luke.* Rev. ed. Anchor Bible Reference Library. New York: Doubleday, 1993.

de Santos Otero, Aurelio. *Los Evangelios Apócrifos.* Madrid: Biblioteca de Autores Cristianos, [6]1988).

Doresse, Jean. "Gnosticism." In *Historia Religionum: Handbook for the History of Religions*, vol. 1, edited by C. J. Bleeker and G. Widengren, 533–579. Leiden: E. J. Brill, 1988.

Ehrman, Bart C. *The Orthodox Corruption of Scripture: The Effect of Early Christological Controversies on the Text of the New Testament*. New York: Oxford University Press, 1993.

Esquinas, José Ramón. *Jesús de Nazaret y su relación con la mujer. Una estudio de género a partir de los evangelios sinópticos*. Vigo: Editorial Academia del Hispanismo, 2007.

Galán, José Gómez. "El nacimiento de Jesús de Nazaret. Historia y cronología." Ph.D. Dissertation. Universidad Complutense de Madrid (April 24, 1998).

Hennecke, Edgar and Wilhelm Schneemelcher. *Neutestamentliche Apokryphen in deutscher Übersetzung*. I Band. Evangelien. Tübingen: J.C.B. Mohr (Paul Siebeck), 1968.

Lipsius, R. A. and M. Bonnet (eds.). *Acta Apostolorum Apocrypha*. Leipzig: Hermann Mendelssohn, 1891-1903, reprod. Wissenschaftliche Buchgesellschaft 1959.

Luz, Ulrich. *Matthew 1–7: A Continental Commentary*. Translated by Wilhelm C. Linss. Minneapolis, MN: Augsburg Fortress, 1989.

Meier, John P. *A Marginal Jew: Rethinking the Historical Jesus*. Vol. 1. New York: Doubleday, 1991.

Merkel, H. "Das geheime Evangelium nach Markus." In *Neutestamentliche Apokryphen*, vol. 1, edited by W. Schneemelcher, 89–92. Tübingen: Mohr, 1988.

Montserrat Torrents, J. *Los gnósticos*. 2 vols. Madrid: Gredos, 1983.

Moraldi, Luigi. *Apocrifi del Nuovo Testmento*. Utet, Torino, 1971.

Piñero, Antonio. *Apócrifos del Antiguo Testamento V*. Madrid: Cristiandad, 1987

———. "Cómo y por qué se formó el Nuevo Testamento: El canon neotestamentario." In *Orígenes del Cristianismo. Antecedentes y primeros pasos*, edited by A. Piñero, 339–400. Córdoba: El Almendro, 1991.

———. *Herod the Great*. Badajoz: Editorial Aeschylus, 2007.

———. "Los Evangelios apócrifos," in *Las fuentes del cristianismo*. Edited by Antonio Piñero. Córdoba: El Almendro, 1992.

———. "Los manuscritos del mar Muerto y el Nuevo Testamento." In *Paganos, judíos y cristianos en los textos de Qumrám*, edited by J. Trebolle, 287–318. Madrid: Trotta, 1999.

——— and E. Gomez Segura (ed.). *El Juicio Final en el cristianismo primitivo y las religiones de su entorno*. Madrid: EDAF, 2010.

——— et al. (eds.). *Textos gnósticos. Biblioteca de Nag Hammadi.* Vol. I: *Tratados filosóficos y cosmológicos*. Vol. II: *Evangelios. Hechos. Cartas*. Vol. III: *Apocalipsis y otros escritos*. Madrid: Trotta, 1997–2003.

Smith, Morton. *Clement of Alexandria and a Secret Gospel of Mark*. Cambridge: Harvard University Press, 1973.

Whiston, William (tr.). *The Works of Josephus: Complete and Unabridged*. Peabody: Hendrickson, 1987.

www.ingramcontent.com/pod-product-compliance
Lightning Source LLC
Chambersburg PA
CBHW021234090426
42740CB00006B/529